A CONVERSAT
English in Everyday Life
Revised Third Edition

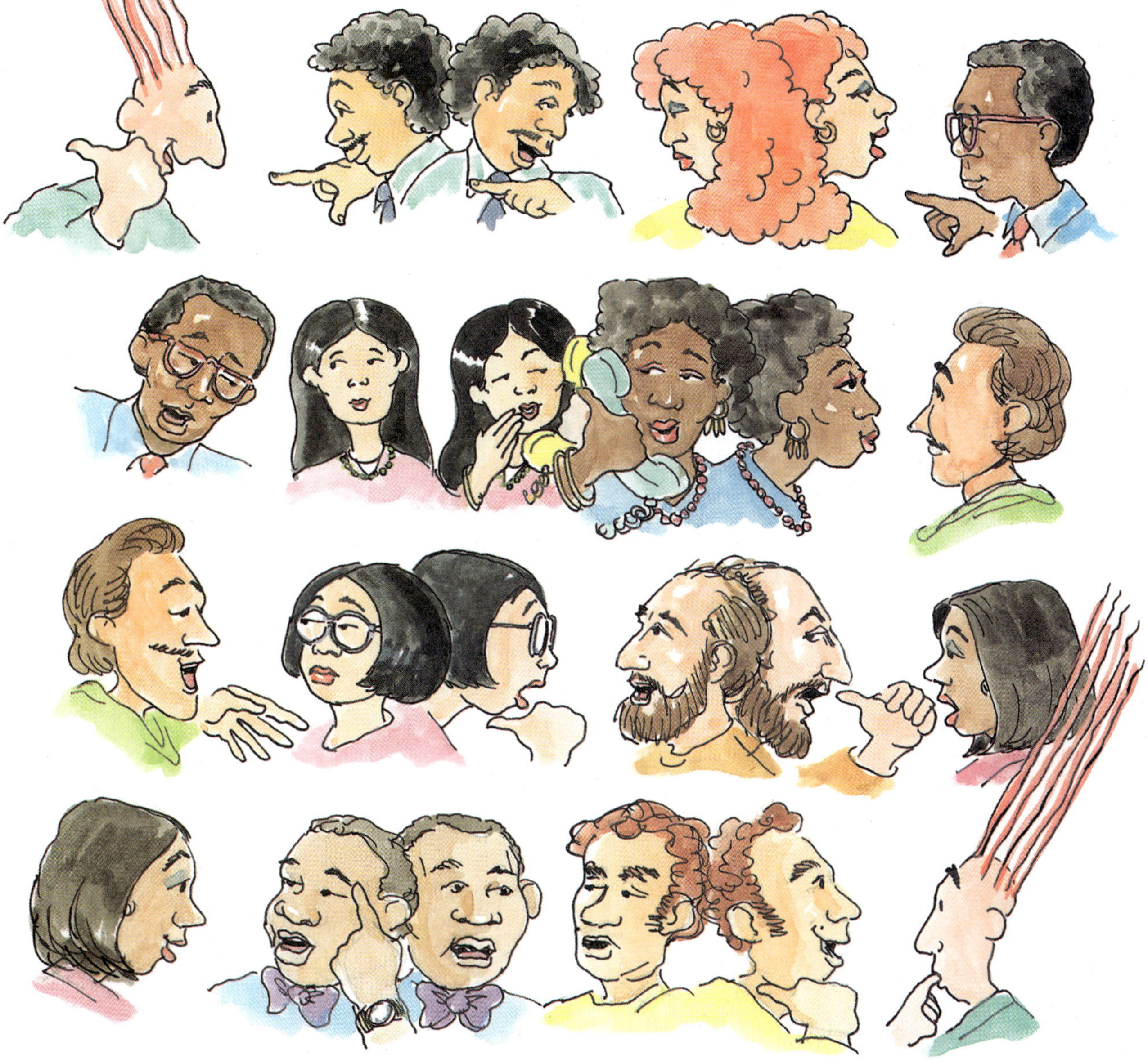

Tina Kasloff Carver
Sandra Douglas Fotinos

Prentice Hall Regents
Upper Saddle River, New Jersey 07458

Publisher: *Louisa B. Hellegers*
Development Editors: *Gino Mastascusa, Barbara Barysh*
Electronic Production Editors: *Christine Mann, Carey Davies*
Michelle LoGerfo

Electronic Art Production Supervisor: *Ken Liao*
Electronic Publishing Specialist: *Steven Greydanus*
Art Director: *Merle Krumper*
Manufacturing Manager: *Ray Keating*

Illustrator: *Andrew Lange*

© 1998 by Prentice Hall Regents
Prentice-Hall, Inc.
A Simon & Schuster Company
Upper Saddle River, New Jersey 07458

All rights reserved. No part of this book may be reproduced, in any form or by any means, without permission in writing from the publisher.

Printed in the United States of America
10 9 8 7 6 5 4 3 2 1

0-13-792458-5

Prentice-Hall International (UK) Limited, *London*
Prentice-Hall of Australia Pty. Limited, *Sydney*
Prentice-Hall Canada Inc., *Toronto*
Prentice-Hall Hispanoamericana, S.A., *Mexico*
Prentice-Hall of India Private Limited, *New Delhi*
Prentice-Hall of Japan, Inc., *Tokyo*
Simon & Schuster Asia Pte. Ltd., *Singapore*
Editora Prentice-Hall do Brasil, Ltda., *Rio de Janeiro*

CONTENTS

FOREWORD ix
ACKNOWLEDGMENTS xi
TO THE TEACHER xiii
TO THE STUDENT xxv

UNIT 1: WELCOME TO CLASS　　1

LESSON	COMPETENCY OBJECTIVES	PAGE
Welcome to Class!	• identify self and others • request and give information	2
Countries	• locate geographical areas	4
Numbers	• learn cardinal numbers • count	6
Journal	• express basic personal information and numbers in written form	7
Clothing and Colors	• identify articles of clothing and colors	8
Pairs of Clothing	• identify pairs of clothing	9
Family	• identify immediate and extended family relationships	10
Review		12

iii

UNIT 2: EVERYDAY LIFE — 13

LESSON	COMPETENCY OBJECTIVES	PAGE
The Classroom	• identify classroom objects	14
Taking a Break	• express feelings and states of being	16
Time	• request time of day • respond to request for time of day	18
Everyday Life	• discuss everyday routine	20
Morning Routine	• discuss morning routine	22
Review		24

UNIT 3: THE CALENDAR 25

LESSON	COMPETENCY OBJECTIVES	PAGE
Days of the Week	• learn the days of the week • make a weekly schedule	26
Months and Dates	• learn ordinal numbers • identify months, dates, year • note dates on a calendar	28
Birthdays	• identify and describe one's birthday	30
Holidays	• identify holidays and discuss their cultural significance	32
Seasons	• discuss seasons of the year and associated activities	34
Weather	• identify and use weather vocabulary	36
Weather Report	• understand forecasts through different media	38
Seasonal Clothing	• identify appropriate clothing for weather conditions	39
Review		40

UNIT 4: FOOD 41

LESSON	COMPETENCY OBJECTIVES	PAGE
Fruit	• identify common fruit	42
Vegetables	• identify common vegetables	44
Meat, Seafood, and Poultry	• identify common meats, seafood, and poultry • describe likes and dislikes	46
Desserts	• identify and express preference for desserts • read a menu	48
Breakfast	• identify breakfast foods • discuss the breakfast meal	50
Lunch	• identify lunch foods • discuss different types of lunches	52
Fast Food	• express preferences for fast food	54
Junk Food	• compare junk food and nutritious food	56
Dinner	• discuss restaurant etiquette • order a meal in a restaurant	57
The Supermarket	• identify items in a supermarket	58
Review		60

UNIT 5: HOMES 61

LESSON	COMPETENCY OBJECTIVES	PAGE
City or Country	• express preference	62
Homes	• identify and describe different types of housing	64
The Kitchen	• identify and describe kitchen appliances and functions of the kitchen	66
The Dining Room	• identify furniture, activities	68
The Living Room	• identify furniture, activities	70
The Bedroom	• identify furniture, activities • tell stories	72
The Bathroom	• identify bathroom items	74
At Home	• identify activities in the home	75
Neighbors	• talk about neighbors • identify problems with neighbors; discuss solutions	76
Problems at Home	• identify problems at home; discuss solutions • complain; request assistance	78
Review		80

UNIT 6: SHOPPING   81

LESSON	COMPETENCY OBJECTIVES	PAGE
Going Shopping!	• identify different stores; what can be purchased	82
Sporting Goods Store	• identify athletic equipment • make decisions	84
Toy Store	• identify toys • make decisions • tell stories	86
Shoe Store	• identify different types of shoes	88
Men's Clothing Store	• identify men's clothing • make decisions	90
Women's Clothing Store	• identify women's clothing • make decisions	91

APPENDIX   93

Conversation Springboards	94
Grammar for Conversation	106
Maps	118
Nations/Nationalities	123
Names/Nicknames	124
Gossip Secrets	125
Speech/Audience Evaluation Forms	125
Alphabetical Word List to Picture Dictionary	126

FOREWORD

The Revised Third Edition of **A CONVERSATION BOOK 1** comes only three years after the Third Edition, in response to requests from many teachers for a split edition. Almost immediately after the Third Edition was published in 1994—featuring a picture dictionary format with a variety of student-centered activities—we started receiving requests for a split edition. Since the book contains so much material, some teachers wanted to spread **A CONVERSATION BOOK 1** lessons over two semesters; others simply wanted more options to choose from. Most also asked for sample conversations and a handy reference section of grammar for conversation.

If you are one of the many teachers who wrote or talked to us, this edition is our response to your requests. If you are not, we hope you will like the changes we have made here to give **A CONVERSATION BOOK** greater flexibility without sacrificing any of the spirit or the content of the original.

The Revised Third Edition is available as either a full edition or a split edition (1A and 1B). Both editions have Conversation Springboards and Grammar for Conversation sections in the Appendix, and the Conversation Springboards as well as the discrete vocabulary are also available on audiotape cassettes.

As with the Third Edition, a page-by-page Teacher's Edition, a separate, duplicatable Testing Program, and boxed, color transparencies are available to supplement the text.

The new edition remains true to the original concept of **A CONVERSATION BOOK**: that students acquire conversation skills best when their own experiences and interests are part of the conversation, and that student-centered, cross-cultural materials with extensive vocabulary and engaging illustrations focused on everyday life can help make the learning process a pleasure. We hope that **A CONVERSATION BOOK 1, REVISED THIRD EDITION** will help to make your conversation class a meaningful, enjoyable, and memorable learning experience for you and your students.

ACKNOWLEDGMENTS

No book is ever written in isolation. We could never begin to cite all the teachers we have spoken with, the programs we have been able to observe, and the authors who have influenced the writing of this book. They all have been part of our education and developing expertise as authors. We are indebted to them all, as well as to those teachers and students who have used the last two editions of the **CONVERSATION BOOK.**

The process of getting a book from first concept to press and out to the classroom involves many people. We were fortunate to have had dedicated, competent support during this time. For the Third Edition, which is the basis of the revised edition, our sincere appreciation goes to Nancy Baxer, our editor. Noël Vreeland Carter, our production editor, combined her remarkable skills in designing and editing with a great sensitivity to ESL and to the visual presentation, which has resulted in a masterfully produced book—both student-friendly and usable. Andrew Lange, our artist, embarked on this venture with an open mind and a wonderful spirit, and has combined his creative artwork with understanding and humor. The result is a whole new artistic pedagogy—a major focus of change in the third edition.

Also, thanks to Barbara Barysh, Andy Martin, and Gil Muller, as well as to H.T. Jennings, Karen Chiang, and Norman Harris, for their professional contributions and personal support. A word of thanks to our reviewers for their assistance in pointing the way to us and for their constructive, helpful, and supportive comments. Thanks to Ann Creighton, Edwina Hoffman, Laurie Ogilvie Lewis, Toni Hadi, Roni Lebauer, Barbara Wiggin, Greg Cossu, Kay Ferrell, and Kedre Murray.

The split editions are the result of a collaborative effort of many people. However, our sincere thanks and great appreciation must go first to Gino Mastascusa, who became our partner in every way. Gino's dedication, creativity, attention to detail, and unflagging long hours and hard work have further improved these texts. No words of thanks are really adequate. Kudos to you, Gino. Barbara Barysh, who helped in so many ways in the third edition, lent a superb editorial eye to this revision by catching so many inconsistencies and suggesting ways to make the materials more easily taught. Thanks also to Janet Johnston for her excellent support in the development of the text.

In a text such as this, production qualities are of utmost importance. The appeal to the student, the "look" as well as the accessibility, contribute to its pedagogy almost as much as the content itself. Christine Mann did a masterful production of the texts, further proving her excellence in her craft. Thanks to Carey Davies, for his additional technical support and extraordinary revisions of the maps.

Our sincere thanks to Louisa Hellegers, our publisher, who took the ideas of the field and helped mold them into reality. Because of Louisa, these texts have been published with the values and the timeliness they needed to serve the market.

Our appreciation goes to Ki Chul Kang, ELT manager in Korea, who for years, gathered information and suggestions from teachers in Asia, and helped mold for us this new revision. Also, Steven Golden, Nancy Baxer, Stephen Troth, Gunawan Hadi, Jerene Tan—thanks for your support both now and over the years.

Our thanks to Professor H. Douglas Brown, who guided us through the Learning Strategies and made great suggestions for our activities.

The list could go on and on—and fearful that we have omitted someone, we thank also Betty Azar, Tom Dare, Mike Bennett, Gordon Johnson, Susan Fesler, Rob Walters, and Maria Angione. Apologies to those we have missed and who also deserve credit!

Our own personal experiences as ESL teachers as well as foreign language learners underlie every page of **A CONVERSATION BOOK 1.** As learners, living and working in other countries, we were reminded daily that learning a new culture and a new language is very hard work! To the many people who have afforded us friendship when we were far from home, helped us deal with the complexity of everyday life in a new place, and patiently shared perceptions and languages with us, thank you. Without those experiences and without those people to guide us, **A CONVERSATION BOOK 1** would never have been written.

A Personal Word from Tina Carver

It is rare that an *editor* is afforded the opportunity to thank *authors*, but this time, the role reversal is appropriate. I have the good fortune to be associated with several people who professionally exhibit the highest level of excellence to which I aspire, and who, through the years, have also become very good friends. I will always value that friendship. So, to Betty Azar, Bill Bliss, Doug Brown, Robert Lado, and Steve Molinsky, thank you—so much of the improvement in this revision is the result of the many years of our professional conversations and work together.

A special note of appreciation goes to Sandra Fotinos, my master teacher of so many years ago, whose expert teaching and instincts towards students' needs have set an example to me throughout my career. Through all these years and experiences, both personal and professional, we have remained friends and colleagues.

I would like to express my appreciation to my three children, Jeffrey, Brian, and Daniel. They were all barely pre-schoolers when the first edition was published. Now college students, they watched over my shoulder as the third edition came to fruition. Their daily help and understanding—from reading the manuscript and offering suggestions to doing the cooking, laundry, shopping, and walking the dogs—made my work easier and, indeed, possible. My mother and father, Ruth and George Kasloff, influenced my early decision-making. My mother has continued to guide and to support me in all my endeavors. Finally, I would like to express my appreciation to Gene Podhurst for his cheerful and helpful contributions. He has read every page of the student text and the Teacher's Edition and the Testing Program over and over—and over—again. His excellent suggestions and insightful comments on the pedagogy and the execution of the ideas have added greatly to the new level of interest and the improvements made in this third edition.

A Personal Word from Sandra Fotinos-Riggs

I would like to thank my colleagues at Cochise College, Northern Essex Community College, and Harvard University for the many good years of stories and teaching techniques that we have shared, and for the constant, gentle reminder that what works once does not necessarily work again in another class or for another teacher.

For whatever I have really learned of living across cultures and languages through the delights and the hard times of everyday life, I want to say thank you to my Fotinos family-by-marriage, and especially to my mother-in-law, Kleopatra Fotinou, of Kallitsaina, Messinias, who has been for over thirty years, my Greek teacher and a loving, understanding friend.

Finally, thank you again to my children, Christina, Elizabeth, and Paul, who, like Tina's children, grew up with the **CONVERSATION BOOKS,** and whose cross-cultural life experiences are imbedded in so many of the conversations of the books. And, for the personal support without which this revision would have been impossible, thank you to Gene Riggs, my incredibly patient husband, and Tina Carver, for twenty-five years my co-author and friend.

New York/Arizona
July 1997

TO THE TEACHER

Our intention in writing **A CONVERSATION BOOK 1** was to provide a wide variety of vocabulary and student-centered learning activities for you to use with your beginning and low intermediate students—within your own style.

Equally important is creating an atmosphere of shared learning in which students' differences are valued and their life experiences are appreciated. Learning a foreign language is perhaps the most threatening of all disciplines yet among the most rewarding. In the conversation class, students need to feel the class is a partnership—one between teacher and student as well as between student and student.

THE FIRST CLASS

The most important goal on the first day of class is to set a supportive, non-threatening learning environment. The room should be pleasant and welcoming; if possible, provide a way of relaxation for the students (who may be quite anxious), such as playing music when they arrive and/or offering coffee and tea and a snack. This will prove to be a worthwhile investment of time and thought.

- Provide name tags for all students (either just first names or both first and last). Wear one yourself.
- Spend time talking with students even before tackling the Welcome to Class! section. (Perhaps you don't even want to use the text during the first class; instead, have an informal, ice-breaking session. Use the *material* of the text but without the text itself.)
- Introduce yourself, speaking slowly. Ask, *"What's your name?"* If a student doesn't understand, use another student as a model, or ask *yourself* and answer it as a model. Try to scout any students who may know a little more and use them as models, too. Write the questions on the board to help students who may recognize written words but not be able to understand what you are saying. As the semester proceeds, both you and your students will learn to understand each other's speech. In the meantime, provide written reinforcement to reduce anxiety.

Suggestion

- Bring a large, lightweight ball to class.
- Have students stand in a circle. Participate in the first round.
- Hold the ball. Say your name and throw the ball to a student (Student 1) you are relatively sure will respond.
- Motion to Student 1 to repeat your name.
- Have Student 1 say his or her name and throw the ball to another student (Student 2) who says Student 1's name. Then as Student 2 throws the ball, he or she says his or her own name.
- Explain *throw* and *catch* by *doing* the actions.
- Repeat the game until all students have had a chance or two to give their own name.
- Do this activity as an entire class or in groups, depending on the size of the class.

This will be a gentle beginning into the more intricate movements of Total Physical Response (TPR) activities.

You will notice a "mascot" throughout the book. Sometimes he is sitting on the vocabulary boxes, sometimes he is integrated into the drawings. You and the class may want to *name* the mascot during the first session. This could be an enjoyable "Name Game." Ask the class to suggest names for him. List the names on the board. Then have the class vote on the names and give him the name the students select.

LEARNING STRATEGIES

The Learning Strategies box on the first page of every unit suggests ways to facilitate learning for the unit. This small section is designed to guide students to understand, appreciate, develop, and broaden their own learning styles. Discuss each strategy with the students as you begin the unit. Have students concentrate on the strategies throughout the unit and have them continue to practice the strategies from previous units. Add strategies as everyone in the class becomes aware of his or her unique learning style.

Read out loud the introduction (To the Student) from Professor H. Douglas Brown and discuss the advantages of understanding how each individual has his or her own way to learn most effectively.

VOCABULARY

Although the lessons in the full as well as the split editions of A CONVERSATION BOOK 1 are designed for use either sequentially or in random order, the words are listed only once—the first time they appear on a text page. Keep this in mind if you are not using the book sequentially, from beginning to end. Every lesson has at least one vocabulary box. The list in the box is *not* exhaustive, but it does give the basic vocabulary for the lesson. Although words are not repeated in the subsequent boxes, the *items* are found repeatedly throughout the text in the illustrations. For example, in the full edition the word **shirt** appears first in the lesson on **Clothing and Colors** (Unit 1). The word does not appear in the vocabulary box in the **Men's Clothing Store** lesson (Unit 6), but a shirt appears in the *illustration* for that lesson. This device can serve as a review. Use the Alphabetical Word List in the Appendix to find the words and their original page references.

We have suggested several ways to present the vocabulary in the **Teacher's Edition**. Ultimately, the best methods depend upon your own style of teaching and the students' style of learning. You may want to discuss the illustration first, using the text or the transparency. This allows students to utilize what they already know and lets you assess the class' level of vocabulary proficiency. It also gives an immediate context for the vocabulary. Alternatively, you can simply point to each illustration and ask for the words. This way students associate the illustration with the English word. Combine methods for variety. Any method loses its effectiveness if used over and over again.

Every vocabulary box has lines for students to write vocabulary they contribute to the class discussion. These can be words students already know or words they want to learn (through a dictionary, other students, or you as the teacher-resource). Make these student-generated words part of the lesson, too.

Modeling the words for pronunciation is useful for students so they can *hear* how to *say* the word in English along with *seeing* the illustration and the *written* word. You can now use the Audio Program for practice in pronouncing the discrete words of each lesson, or model the words you see. Although sometimes it is difficult for you to hear all the pronunciations, choral repetition will give all students an opportunity to verbalize the words they are learning. Be sure students understand all the words. Sometimes native language translation is appropriate; that is your judgment call!

NOTE TAKING

Suggest that students buy a notebook. Have students divide the notebook into four sections: **Vocabulary, Activities, Journal, Community Information**. When new words are generated in the classroom from discussion or from activities, students should record the words and information in the **Vocabulary** section of their notebooks. Write new words on the board for students to record more easily. The **Activities** section should be used for any activities the students do in class or at home. The **Journal** section can be used for additional Journal writing.

The **Community Information** section should be a place to note valuable information about the students' communities. There are specific suggestions in the **Teacher's Edition** as to how and when to use the notebook.

CONVERSATION SPRINGBOARDS

Here are dialogs for teachers who hate dialogs! We have developed these springboards as conversation starters, to serve as models and inspirations for students to talk about their life experiences. They are not designed to be used for pattern practice! They are intentionally longer than traditional dialogs because they are meant for listening to and understanding real, whole conversations about everyday life in English. An accompanying Audio Program is available, which includes all of these Conversation Springboards.

Cassette icons 🎧 on student-text pages signal where to use the audiotape. Each icon is footnoted with a cross-reference to the **Appendix** page with the corresponding Conversation Springboard.

There are five types of Conversation Springboards: *What's the process?*, *What's happening?*, *What happened?*, *What's next?*, and *What's your opinion?* Each type has a specific purpose.

- *What's the process?* Conversation Springboards are to be used *before* specified activities, and are intended to help students understand and talk about the purpose and process of the activity, as well as possible complications and their solutions.
- *What's happening?* Conversation Springboards tell a story, happening in the present. These dialogs are intended to help students listen to conversational narratives in present time, and to retell stories chronologically, using present and present progressive tenses.
- *What happened?* Conversation Springboards relate a story that happened in the past, and give students practice listening to past-time narratives and retelling the events in order, using past tenses.
- *What's next?* Conversation Springboards tell a story without an ending, or with a next step implied but not stated. They give students practice in drawing conclusions from indirect information, as well as opportunities to create their own endings in future time.
- *What's your opinion?* Conversation Springboards present a situation where preferences and opinions are expressed, and give students opportunities to agree or disagree with them, express their own opinions, and participate in a class discussion of a topic.

We suggest this method of using the Conversation Springboards and accompanying Audio Program:

1. Listen to the entire conversation once, with books either open or closed, depending on the class level and preference.
2. Listen again, breaking up the conversation by stopping the tape after every two lines. Check for understanding. Define any words that are unclear. Whenever possible, have students write down unclear words and try to guess the meaning from context.
3. Listen to the entire dialog again. (If you have listened with books closed until now, listen with books open this time.)
4. Follow up by having students either explain the process, situation, or problem, or tell the story of the conversation, depending on which type of Conversation Springboard you are using.
5. You may wish to have students read the conversations out loud themselves, depending on the class level and preference. If you do, go slowly! Remember that these are beginning students and long conversations!

GRAMMAR FOR CONVERSATION

The Grammar for Conversation section of the Appendix consists of conversation–based grammar charts and lists for each unit. The charts focus on basic grammar constructions and lists of formulaic expressions that students need to use extensively in each unit. The grammar emerges from the conversations and activities in the unit and the Conversation Springboards.

The conversations in this book are not grammar based. On the contrary, the practical needs of conversation in everyday life form the basis of the grammar included in the text. As a result, many grammar constructions appear very early in the book. They are intended to serve as springboards for understanding and using grammar in the context of everyday conversation, not for studying the grammar of English in a more conventional, systematic way. Each grammar element in a chart or list appears only once in the **Appendix**, although the same grammar element can occur throughout the book. Thus, students should be encouraged to refer to grammar charts from early units continually throughout the semester. You might want to teach and/or review a particular construction for an activity before or after the activity. However, the emphasis should be on conversation and communication, not grammatical accuracy.

In keeping with the **CONVERSATION BOOK** philosophy, the Conversation Springboards and Grammar for Conversation serve as beginnings—ways to get started listening and talking with the class, and ways to spark individual thinking and creativity. English may be a new language to your students, but that newness should not prevent them from using it creatively and having fun in the process of learning it. Most of all, have fun with these conversations!

CORRECTIONS

Use your own best judgment in handling corrections. Too much correction inhibits students' ability to think coherently and works contrary to practicing coherent and fluent conversation skills. On the other hand, aim to strike a balance, teaching syntax as well as pronunciation at opportune times. Take note of the errors students are making. It is usually not helpful to interrupt the flow of students' conversations, but correct errors at the appropriate time later in class, without referring to any specific students.

GROUPING

Pairing partners can be done in a variety of ways. The easiest way is to have students seated next to each other be partners. However, since an objective of the partner activities is for students to get to know one another, having a variety of partners is essential. Pairing students in different ways maintains students' attention, moves them around the room, and helps them to learn each other's names.

Suggestion:

- Count the students in the class; then divide them in half by left side/right side or front/back.
- Hand out slips of paper to one half of the students.
- Ask them to write their full names on the paper and fold the paper.
- Collect all the folded papers, then walk through the other half of the class. Have each student pick one folded paper.
- When all the papers are handed out, instruct the students with the papers to find their partners and sit down together.
- Depending on the class (and your own teaching style), you may prefer an open free-for-all with everyone walking around at once, calling out names; or a more structured pairing may be more appropriate in which one student at a time reads the name on his or her paper. The student named raises his or her hand, and the two then sit together.

These methods of pairing can be used again and again, dividing the class in different ways to assure that students have many different partners and get to know everyone in the class by name.

Partners should always ask each other for their names; there is a place in each **Partner Activity** for students to write their **Partner's Name**.

For some activities, larger groups of students are necessary. Again, grouping students can be done in a variety of ways.

Suggestion:
- Have students count off numbers (1–4, 1–5, 1–6, etc.), then join those who have that number.
- To practice vocabulary, you may replace numbers with items from the current vocabulary list—colors, fruits, vegetables, flowers, seasons, etc.
- List the group names on the board (for example, with colors, Red, Black, Yellow, Green, etc.), then assign each student a color and have students form groups according to their assigned color.

After students get to know each other, informal methods of pairing or grouping usually work best. Sometimes you can let students choose a partner or set up their own groups. For other activities, depending on the subject matter, you may want to deliberately mix gender, ages, language groups, occupations, or opinions. Try to avoid cliques sitting together. Remind students that the only way to develop conversational fluency in English is to practice *in English*.

PARTNER ACTIVITIES

Partner activities give students non-threatening, one-on-one opportunities to interact on a personal level. They are the only activities in which every student in the class has to do 50% of the talking and has to listen on a one-on-one basis. We have included four types of partner activities: **Games, Interviews, Journals,** and **Role Plays**.

Games

There are two types of partner games: **Memory Games** and **Mime Games**. Always do a "dry run" with the class to make sure that students understand the task.

Memory Games
What Do You Remember?
- Divide the class into pairs.
- Have the class look at the illustration. Show the transparency. Discuss how to remember the details of the illustration as they are looking at it (how many people, what are the colors, what season is it, what activities do you see, etc.).
- Then have the students close their texts and turn to the **Activities** section of their notebooks.
- Have the pairs work together, brainstorming everything they remember about the illustration. Have each pair make one list and number each item so that it will be easy to count how many items they listed.
- When students have finished, encourage several pairs to dictate the things they remember as you write them on the board. Or have one of the partners write the list on the board. Give several students the opportunity to do this.
- Open the texts or show the transparency. Look at the illustration together.
- Draw a line under the last item listed and have students dictate additional items as you write them on the board.
- Point out new vocabulary for students to add to the **Vocabulary** section of their notebooks.

Same or Different?

- Divide the class into pairs.
- Have students study the illustrations they are going to compare. Show the transparency.
- Instruct the pairs to make one list of similarities and differences in the illustrations.
- Remind students to number each item so it will be easy to count how many items they listed.
- While students are working, write two horizontal headings: SAME and DIFFERENT.
- When students have finished their lists, have several pairs dictate their lists as you write the items on the board.
- Open the texts or show the transparency. Look at the illustrations together.
- Draw a line under the last item listed. Have students dictate additional items as you write them on the board.
- Point out new vocabulary for students to add to the **Vocabulary** section of their notebooks.

Vocabulary Challenges

- Divide the class into pairs.
- Books must be closed. "Challenge" pairs of students to make a list of as many vocabulary words and phrases as they remember from the lesson. Remind them to number the words as they write. Give them a time limit for completing the list.
- When the time is up, ask how many words and phrases each pair had.
- Have a pair read their entire list or copy it on the board. Star ★ the words that are *not* from the lesson. Have the class check off the words they have on their lists.
- Have another pair read *only* the words they have that *aren't* on the board. List the new words on the board. Double-star ★★ the new words.
- Have the class check off the words they have that are on the board.
- Have another pair read *new* words from their list. List the new words on the board. Triple-star ★★★ the new words. Have the class check off any words they have on their lists.
- Ask which pair has other new words. Add the words to the list.
- Ask which pair had the most new words. They "win" the challenge!

Mime Games

Sometimes students are asked to act out words or actions with a partner. Demonstrate the activity for the students first so they understand what to do. As the class is doing the activity, circulate; help as needed.

Interviews

It is important, especially during the first days of class, for the students to understand how to conduct these interviews. Your role is to model pronunciation, facilitate understanding of vocabulary and questions, and provide possible answers. For modeling, use a student who will catch on quickly; be careful not to use the same student all the time. Or, if it is more appropriate, model both roles yourself. Write the question and answer on the board so that students can *see* the questions and answers as well as *hear* them.

- Practice the interview questions with the students. Be sure they understand the questions and the vocabulary. Supply any additional words needed.
- Divide the class into pairs.
- Have students interview their partners. Circulate; help as needed.
- After partners conduct their interviews, have several pairs present their interviews to the class. Either have them present all questions or have different pairs present one question each. Alternatively, have them share what they have learned with another pair of students.

- Write new vocabulary generated from the interviews on the board. Have students copy the new words in the **Vocabulary** section of their notebooks.
- Use the students' responses to the interviews for further discussions which may be of interest to the class.

Journals

The journal entries give students a chance to use the vocabulary and phrases they have learned in writing reinforcement activities. Journals should be done as an interactive activity.

- Discuss the topic with the students before they begin to write.
- Model and practice the questions provided at the top of the page. Add your own questions, if appropriate.
- Divide the class into pairs.
- Have partners ask each other the questions. Circulate; help as needed.
- Have students do their individual journal writing in class or at home.
- Have students proofread their journals.
- Instruct partners to read their journals to each other; encourage them to ask questions and make comments.
- If there is time, have several students read their journals to the class.
- Alternatively, read several journals to the class and have students guess who wrote them.
- Have one or two students put their journal entries on the board. Write the skeleton paragraph as it appears in the text. Either you or the student can fill in the blanks. Have students read what they wrote on the board, or you can read it as a model. Discuss new vocabulary and new ideas.
- Take advantage of any additional topics or information that may emerge to continue conversations and exchanges of information.
- Students can keep more journal pages in the **Journal** section of their notebooks. Provide guidance for the topics and do light corrections. The object of journal pages is for students to have practice writing fluently in English and expressing their thoughts and emotions. Too much correction will inhibit this goal.

Role Plays

Before students do role-playing for the first time, do a sample role play using yourself and another student. This will provide a model for students when they are working independently.

- Divide the class into pairs.
- List the vocabulary needed on the board. Leave the vocabulary on the board as a reference for students when they are working with their partners.
- Students should write the conversation and practice reading their "scripts" with the "read and look up" technique. (*Have the students scan the line and remember it as well as they can; then have them look at the other person and SAY the line without READING it—even beginners can perfect this technique. The appropriate eye contact and body language required in English enhances this technique.*)
- Have several pairs present their role plays—with simple props, if appropriate.
- Encourage the pairs to come to the front of the room or sit in the middle of the circle rather than remain at their desks.
- For classes with shy students, an alternative to a traditional role play is a puppet show. Make hand puppets from small paper bags. Cover a table with a sheet for a stage. This activity can be simple or elaborate.

GROUP ACTIVITIES

Group activities give students a feeling of belonging and a feeling of being a part of the group's success. These activities allow students to get to know one another and to cooperate within the framework of different tasks. Many of the activities are cooperative; they require each member of the group to contribute something. While the groups are working, you can move from group to group as a facilitator to be sure students understand their task. After the groups complete the activity, have them report back to the class as a whole so that a summation and conclusions can be drawn. We have included seven types of group activities: **Conversation Squares, Discussions, Gossip Games, Problem Posing/Problem Solving, Surveys, Vocabulary Challenges,** and **What's the Story?**

Conversation Squares

- Have the students help you create the question they will need to ask for each square.
- Write the questions on the board.
- Construct boxes on the board similar to the ones in the text.
- Choose two students. Use yourself as the third member of the group.
- Put the three names on the top of the boxes as indicated in the text.
- Ask and answer the questions for your box; write in your responses.
- Ask your "partners" the questions. Write in their responses.
- Then ask the class the questions for more practice.
- Have groups of three do the activity.
- When all students have finished, ask different groups single questions from the conversation squares. Put new vocabulary on the board for students to write in the **Vocabulary** section of their notebooks.

Discussions

These activities consist of guided questions. Each group should appoint a *leader* to ask the questions and a *recorder* to record the answers. That way, when called upon to recite, the answers are written down and students can feel confident in their replies. Real learning in these activities goes on within the group's dynamic. Reporting back is a way to summarize. Students shouldn't feel intimidated by the reporting back part of the activity. Writing answers usually eliminates this anxiety.

During the "reporting back" stage, note new vocabulary, write it on the board, and have students write the new words in the **Vocabulary** section of their notebooks.

Gossip!

This is a variation of the "Gossip" or "Telephone" game. It has two objectives: to practice new vocabulary in context without visual cues and to demonstrate how information is lost in the process of retelling. A *secret* for each game is included in the **Appendix**.

- Divide the class into large groups, or do this activity with the whole class, if your class is small.
- Use the illustration on the text's cover to explain the game. Start on the top left with the mascot. End on the bottom right with the mascot.
- Have the *leader* from each group read the *secret* silently several times. All other students should have their books closed.
- Be sure to explain the words "whisper" and "secret." Have the *leaders* close their books and quietly whisper the *secret* to the student next to them. Those students quietly whisper it to the next, and so on.
- When all students have heard the *secret*, have the last student of each group report the information to the class, either orally or in written form on the board.
- Have everyone read the *secret* together to see what information was lost and changed.

Problem Posing/Problem Solving

- Divide the class into small groups.
- Do a practice Problem Posing/Problem Solving example with the class as a whole.

- Have each group choose a *recorder* and a *leader*. Each student should participate in some way.
- Before students begin, be sure that they understand the goal of the activity and that they have adequate vocabulary and grammar to do the work.
- Have students think about what is happening in the illustration and formulate a question about it (pose the problem). Remind the *leader* to ask the questions.
- Then have them think through (analyze) the problem and make a group decision as to what to do (solve the problem). This will take thought, negotiation, resolution, and consensus.
- To summarize, have each *recorder* report back to the class.
- Draw class conclusions, even if there is diversity of opinion and no real resolution.

Surveys

This activity gives students the opportunity to express their own opinions and preferences, and check their accuracy in listening and recording answers.
- Model the questions; have students repeat; check pronunciation.
- Be sure students understand all the vocabulary and the objective of the activity before the activity begins.
- Have students check off their own answers in the appropriate column.
- Divide the class into groups of seven to ten. If your class is small, do the activity with the whole class.
- Encourage the students to get up and walk around while asking questions. Remind them that each student should ask everyone in the group all the questions and check the appropriate column for every answer.
- Set a time limit. Tell students to sit down when they finish and count their results. Remind them to include their own answers in the count.
- Have students report their results to their group. If other members of the group have different numbers, have them figure out who is right.
- While groups are working, copy the chart on the board.
- When groups are sure of their numbers, have them report their results. Fill in the columns on the board and have students draw conclusions about the class.
- Point out new words and have students write them in the **Vocabulary** section of their notebooks.

Vocabulary Challenges

This activity is similar to the **Vocabulary Challenges** as described in the **Memory Games** section of **PARTNER ACTIVITIES**.

What's the Story?

The goal of this activity is to have students look at an illustration (which tells a story), then use their imaginations and the vocabulary they know to create their own story. These activities are cooperative learning activities. Each student should contribute one, two, or three lines. The story should be complete and make sense.
- Divide the class into groups.
- Have each group select a *recorder* to write everyone's lines.
- Encourage students to help each other. Be sure that even the shy students participate by contributing their lines.
- After the stories are written, all groups should listen to their *recorder* read the story. They should all make changes and corrections and "edit" the story before the rest of the class hears it. Have another student (*not* the *recorder*) read the story, or have each student read or recite his or her lines, or part of the narrative.
- Have the class decide which was the best, the most exciting, the saddest, the funniest, etc.

CLASS ACTIVITIES

Class activities provide opportunities for lots of input; this is the advantage of a large class. Many opinions and answers make the class more interesting and exciting. However, if your class functions better in smaller groups, these activities can work as Group Activities also. We have included seven types of class activities: **Community Activities, Cross-Cultural Exchanges, Discussions, Find Someone Who, Strip Stories, Total Physical Response (TPR) Activities,** and **Vocabulary Challenges.**

Community Activities

These activities give the class the opportunity to venture into the community and explore, as well as to discover community resources (for example, the telephone book) in the classroom itself. Students can be sent out individually, in groups, or with partners to gather information requested.

- Review the task before students are asked to do the work independently. Be sure students know the vocabulary and are clear about what they are to do.
- To help prepare students, role-play expected scenarios and outcomes. This may avoid pitfalls and panic!
- If possible, accompany the class the first time out. This will give them confidence.
- After the students do the assignment, review it in class.
- Discuss not only the task but what happened—what surprises they had, what reactions they had, how they felt, etc.
- Have students keep important community information in the **Community** section of their notebooks.

Cross-Cultural Exchanges

These activities give the class the opportunity to talk about cultural differences in general as well as about U.S./Canadian cultures. Students should be encouraged to voice their opinions and confusions about cultures they associate with the English language. Opportunities and interest in this activity will vary with your classes. Wherever possible, compare three or more cultures rather than just two to avoid potential "either/or" interpretations of differences. Encourage intercultural openness and awareness without judgment.

Discussion

Ask the guided questions and choose different students to answer each question. This provides a model for the students. As an alternative approach, you can ask the first question and choose a student to answer. Then have that student ask the second question and choose a student to answer. Continue the pattern. Correct only large errors that impede understanding.

To help structure discussions and teach note-taking skills, write a brief heading for each question on the board. Encourage students to do the same in the **Activities** section of their notebooks. List information you gather from the discussions under each heading. Then review your notes and ask the students to review theirs. Draw conclusions together from the notes at the end of the discussion.

Find Someone Who

This activity is similar to the **Survey** activity, except in this activity, students are searching for "Yes" answers.

- Review the vocabulary and create the Yes/No questions with the class before they start the activity. Write the questions on the board.
- Give students the grammar constructions in chunks. Review appropriate grammar from the **Appendix**.

- Have the class ask the questions by circulating around the class. If the class is very large, break the class into groups of 10–15 and have students do the activity within their group.
- When students have completed their work, have them sit in their seats.
- Review the questions and answers. There should be interesting "springboards of conversation" that come from the individual answers.

Strip Stories

This visual presentation of little stories gives students the opportunity to discuss the action in the frames and then to write their own captions.
- Have students look at the illustrations and discuss them together.
- Write vocabulary words on the board.
- Ask for suggestions for captions and/or bubbles.
- Write different suggestions on the board. Have students decide which one is best and why.
- Have students write captions in their texts.
- Alternatively, have students create captions individually, in groups, or with partners.

Total Physical Response (TPR) Activities

The first Total Physical Response (TPR) activity has illustrations for each of the steps. (See page 5 of the full edition.) After that, only the *instructions* for TPR activities appear in the text.
- Prepare students by giving out slips of paper that they will write something on—an instruction, a favorite month, a favorite food, etc.
- Always model the action before asking students to do it. The object of this activity is for students to associate the action with the words for it. Use exaggerated movements.
- After you demonstrate the action, have the class repeat that action.
- To review, have a student read the action and have the class follow the instruction.
- As a written review, dictate the action and have students write the dictation in the **Activities** section of their notebooks.

Vocabulary Challenges

This activity is similar to the **Vocabulary Challenges** as described in the **Memory Games** section of **PARTNER ACTIVITIES**.

INDIVIDUAL ACTIVITIES

These activities are designed for students to have the opportunity to share their individual perceptions, knowledge, and experiences with the whole class. There are three types of individual activities: **Draw, Speeches,** and **Tell the Class.**

Draw

Students don't have to be artists—nor do you—to do this. A rendition of what is called for is good enough for students to be able to talk about the drawing.
- Give students enough time to complete their drawing.
- Circulate; help as needed, but also scout students who will be able to share a useful drawing—either on the board, as a transparency, or with photocopies.
- Use your own artwork—the "worse" it is, sometimes, the better. Students are less reluctant to share theirs if yours *isn't* "good"!
- Have students talk about what they drew. Be sure to note new vocabulary words.

Speeches

Students get practice in simple speech writing and recitation with these activities. Give students ample time to prepare. Make the activity *very* structured and help correct as much as you can. Visual aids can help relieve anxiety. Allow students to have note cards, but not to read their speech. Sometimes it is helpful for students to practice with a partner or a small group before addressing the class. There are **Speech** and **Audience Evaluation Forms** in the **Appendix**.

Tell the Class

These activities give students the opportunity to be in front of the class and speak without much preparation. With some notes, a little confidence, and a supportive environment, their anxiety levels will be lowered.

TEACHER'S EDITION

The **Teacher's Edition**, interleaved with actual student-text pages, provides the teacher a convenient teaching tool. The format is easy to follow: **Warm Up** activities for each lesson precede the step-by-step suggestions for all **In the Text** activities. Objectives are clearly stated for each lesson. In addition, there is a wide variety of **Expansion** activities for each lesson. The **To the Teacher** section gives an overview of all activities and objectives.

TESTING PROGRAM

This program includes both conversation and vocabulary tests for each unit. Suggestions for administration with large and small classes are included. Permission to photocopy the tests is granted.

TRANSPARENCIES

A boxed set of **Color Transparencies** is available. These transparencies include *all* the illustrations from the picture dictionary pages as well as other illustrations which lend themselves to class discussions and activities. The transparencies can facilitate the introduction of the vocabulary lesson by allowing students to close their books and look up, rather than being engrossed in words and page turning. The transparencies focus students' attention and enable teachers to point out details more easily. The transparencies can also be used for class activities, for vocabulary review, and as an alternative testing instrument.

TO THE STUDENT

In **A CONVERSATION BOOK 1**, your teacher will help you to learn English by using it in conversations with English speakers. Your work in the classroom is very important. It will help you to practice English, to speak more clearly and fluently, and to listen to others carefully and understand what they are saying. But it is also very important for you to practice English *outside* of the classroom.

To help you to be a better learner of English, I have ten "rules" for successful language learning that I encourage you to follow. These rules suggest ways to help you become a successful learner. If you can follow this advice, you too will learn English more successfully. Here are the ten rules:

1. Don't be afraid!

Sometimes we are afraid to speak a foreign language because we think we are going to make terrible mistakes and people will laugh at us. Well, the best learners of foreign languages try not to be afraid. They make a "game" of learning. They are not anxious about making mistakes. And they sometimes share their fears with friends. You can do that, too, and you will then feel better about yourself.

2. Dive in!

Try to speak out! Try to say things in English! The best way to learn English is to speak it yourself. Don't worry about perfect pronunciation or grammar; other people usually will not criticize you.

3. Believe in yourself.

You have lots of strengths. You have already learned some English. You must believe that you *can* do it! Compliment your fellow learners on their efforts. Then maybe they will return the favor!

4. Develop motivation.

Why are you learning English? Make a list of your reasons for studying English. Those reasons can be your individual goals for this course. If you have your own reasons for learning English, you will have better success.

5. Cooperate with your classmates.

You are learning language in order to communicate with other people. So, practice with other people and you will be more successful. Create your own conversation group outside of class. Try out new ways to communicate in those groups. And, in class, remember your classmates are your "team" members, not your opponents.

6. Get the "big" picture!

Sometimes learners look too closely at all the details of language (words, pronunciation, grammar, usage). It's OK to pay attention to those details, but it is also important to understand general meanings (the "big" picture). Maybe you don't know all the right words or grammar, but you can say things, anyway. See movies in English. Read books and magazines for pleasure.

7. Don't worry if you're confused.

Learning English is a big task! Sometimes you will feel confused about all the things you have to learn in a foreign language. Try not to worry about everything all at once. Don't try to learn *all* the rules right now. Ask your teacher questions about English. And try to learn a little every day.

8. Trust your "hunches."

Sometimes people think they should analyze everything in their new language (grammar rules, word definitions). The best learners do some analyzing, but they follow their "hunches" (their best guesses, their intuitions) about the new language. If they have an intuition that something sounds right, they will try it. So, the next time you "feel" that something is right, say it. You'll probably be right, and, if you aren't, someone will give you some feedback.

9. Make your mistakes work FOR you.

A mistake is not always "bad." We all make mistakes learning anything new. Successful learners don't worry about mistakes; they learn from them. They take note of their errors and try to correct them the next time. Some things you can do:

- Make a list of your most common mistakes.
- Select grammar points to watch for.
- Tape-record yourself and listen for errors.

10. Set your own goals.

Teachers usually set goals (assignments, homework, classwork) for you. But *you* need to set your own goals, too. You can do that by doing the following:

- Set aside a certain number of hours a week for extra study.
- Learn a certain number of words a day/week.
- Read a certain number of extra pages a day/week.

Take charge of your own learning!

Try to follow at least some of these rules for successful language learning as you work with **A CONVERSATION BOOK 1**. I am sure that you will be a more efficient learner of English, and you will feel proud of your accomplishments. Good luck!

H. Douglas Brown, Ph.D.
American Language Institute
San Francisco State University
San Francisco, CA
May 1997

A CONVERSATION BOOK 1A
English in Everyday Life
Revised Third Edition

UNIT 1

WELCOME TO CLASS

Welcome to Class!	2
Countries	4
Numbers	6
Journal	7
Clothing and Colors	8
Pairs of Clothing	9
Family	10
Review	12

LEARNING STRATEGIES

▶ Introduce yourself to your classmates. Learn their names and your teacher's name. Write them down. After class, introduce yourself to other speakers and learners of English.

▶ Start a notebook. Divide it into sections:
Vocabulary
Activities
Journal
Community Information

WELCOME TO CLASS!

Draw

Draw a picture of yourself.

1. bald	7. brown	10. earrings	16. hair	22. short	_____
2. beard	8. curly	11. eyes	17. long	23. single	_____
3. black	9. divorced	12. girl	18. man	24. straight	_____
4. blond		13. glasses	19. married	25. wavy	_____
5. blue		14. gray	20. moustache	26. widowed	_____
6. boy		15. green	21. name	27. woman	_____

Write

My name is _____.

1. I am a _____.
2. I am _____.
3. My hair is _____.
4. My eyes are _____.
5. I have _____.

See Conversation Springboards on page 94.

Tell the Class*

Write your first name and your last name on the board. • *Tell the class your name.* • *Show your picture to the class.* • *Describe your picture.*

Partner Activity   Partner's Name _____

Introduce yourself to your partner. • *Practice all these ways.*

    A: My name is _____. What's your name? *(or)*
        Hello. I'm _____. What's your name? *(or)*
        Hi. I'm _____. What is your name?

    B: Nice to meet you. My name is _____. *(or)*
        I'm _____. I'm pleased to meet you.

Introduce your partner to the class.

      I'd like you to meet _____. *(or)*
      This is _____.

Group Activity

Work in groups of three or four. • *Write a name tag for yourself.* • *Pronounce the names of each student in your group.* • *Introduce yourself to the others in the group.*

* *See Appendix page 124 for Names/Nicknames.*

COUNTRIES

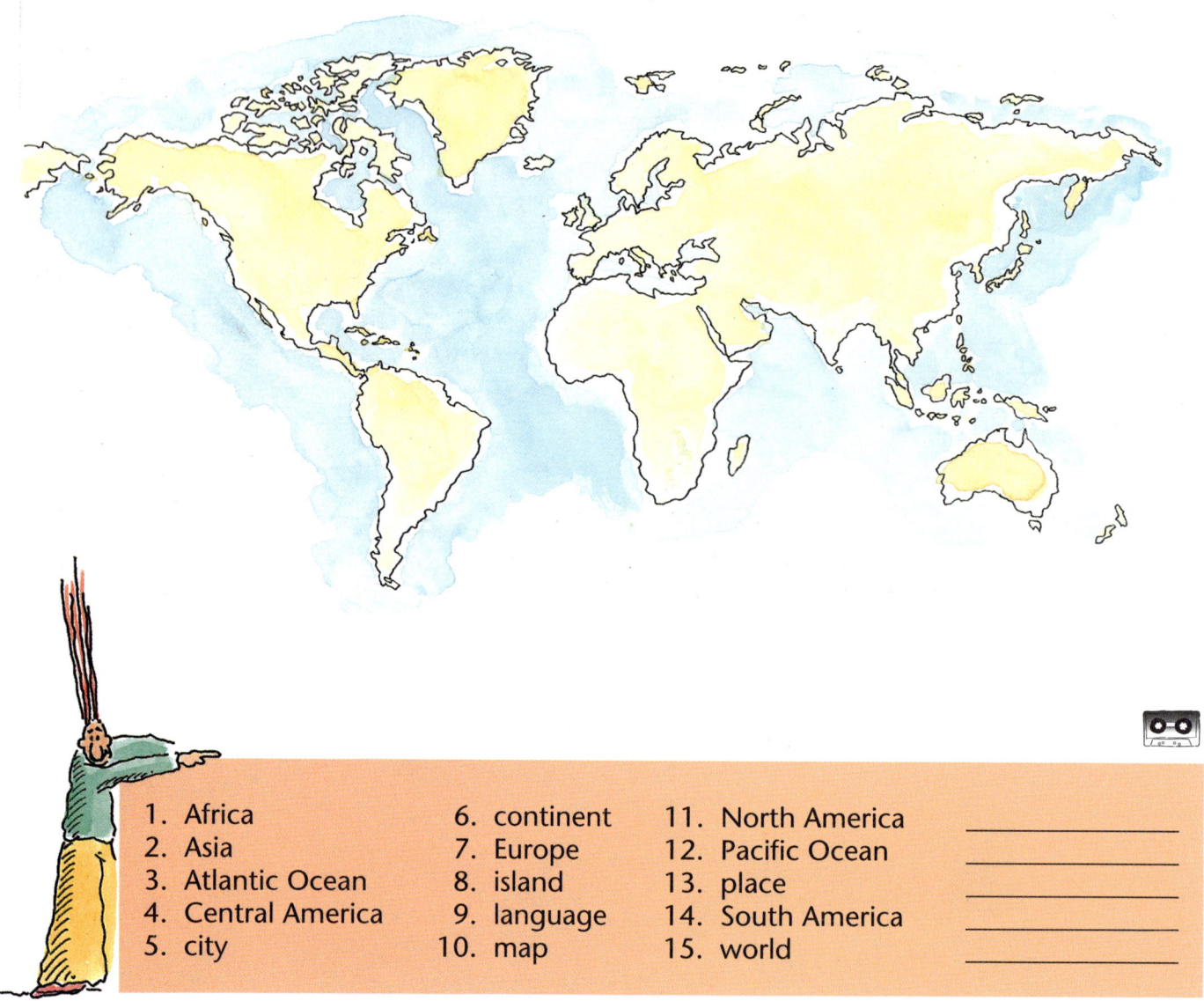

1. Africa
2. Asia
3. Atlantic Ocean
4. Central America
5. city
6. continent
7. Europe
8. island
9. language
10. map
11. North America
12. Pacific Ocean
13. place
14. South America
15. world

Class Activity

Find your country on the map. • *Circle the places on the map where all your classmates are from.*
• *Draw a big star where you are now.*

Partner Interview *

Partner's Name _____

Practice these questions with your teacher. • *Then ask your partner.*

1. What is your name?
2. What country are you from?
3. What city are you from?
4. What continent are you from?
5. Where do you live now?
6. What languages do you speak?

Tell the Class

Tell the class about your partner.

See Conversation Springboards on page 94.

* See Appendix page 123 for Nations/Nationalities.

Class Game*: "Where do you want to visit?"

1. Think.

2. Write.

3. Fold.

4. Make a pile.

5. Open one. Read it to the class.

6. Guess who wrote it.

Tell the Class
Tell the class about the place you want to visit.

* *See Appendix pages 118-122 for Maps.*

NUMBERS

count	8 eight	17 seventeen	26 twenty-six	
0 zero	9 nine	18 eighteen	27 twenty-seven	
1 one	10 ten	19 nineteen	28 twenty-eight	
2 two	11 eleven	20 twenty	29 twenty-nine	
3 three	12 twelve	21 twenty-one	30 thirty	80 eighty
4 four	13 thirteen	22 twenty-two	40 forty	90 ninety
5 five	14 fourteen	23 twenty-three	50 fifty	100 one hundred
6 six	15 fifteen	24 twenty-four	60 sixty	_____
7 seven	16 sixteen	25 twenty-five	70 seventy	_____

Class Survey

Count the men and women in your class. • Write the correct number and word for each question. • What did you find?

	MEN	WOMEN
1. How many are there?	_____	_____
2. How many have  ?	_____	_____
3. How many are  ?	_____	_____
4. How many have blue 👀 ?	_____	_____
5. How many have 👂 ?	_____	_____
6. How many have 👓 ?	_____	_____
7. How many have a 🧔 ?	_____	_____
TOTALS	_____	_____

Group Activity

Work in groups of four. • Write the names of all the students in your group. • Write what you remember about each student. • Compare notes with your group. • Read your group's list to the class.

See Conversation Springboards on page 94.

JOURNAL

Partner Interview

Partner's Name _____

Practice these questions with your teacher.
Then ask your partner.

1. What's today's date?
2. How many students are in our class?
3. What is your name?
4. What color is your hair?
5. What color are your eyes?
6. Are you married or single?
7. Where are you from?
8. What language do you speak?

Write

Write about your partner.

Journal

_____
(1)

I am in my English class. There are _____ students
(2)

in my class today. My partner's name is _____.
(3)

She/He has _____ hair and _____ eyes.
(4) (5)

My partner is _____. She/He is from _____ and
(6) (7)

speaks _____.
(8)

Tell the Class

Read your journal to the class. • *Tell the class about your partner.*

See Conversation Springboards on page 94.

CLOTHING AND COLORS

1. barrette	7. dress	13. purple	19. skirt	25. T-shirt
2. belt	8. gold	14. raincoat	20. sports coat	26. white
3. blouse	9. handkerchief	15. red	21. suit	27. yellow
4. button	10. jacket	16. scarf	22. sweater	28. zipper
5. coat	11. pink	17. shirt	23. sweatshirt	_____
6. collar	12. pocket	18. silver	24. tie	_____

Partner Game: *"What do you remember?"*   **Partner's Name** _____

Look at your partner's clothing. • Sit back to back. • Make a list of what your partner is wearing. • Read your list to your partner. • Don't look at your partner. • Correct your list with your partner.

Class Activity

List on the board the different colors the students are wearing. • How many men are wearing each color? • How many women are wearing each color? • What is the class' favorite color?

See Conversation Springboards on page 94.

PAIRS OF CLOTHING

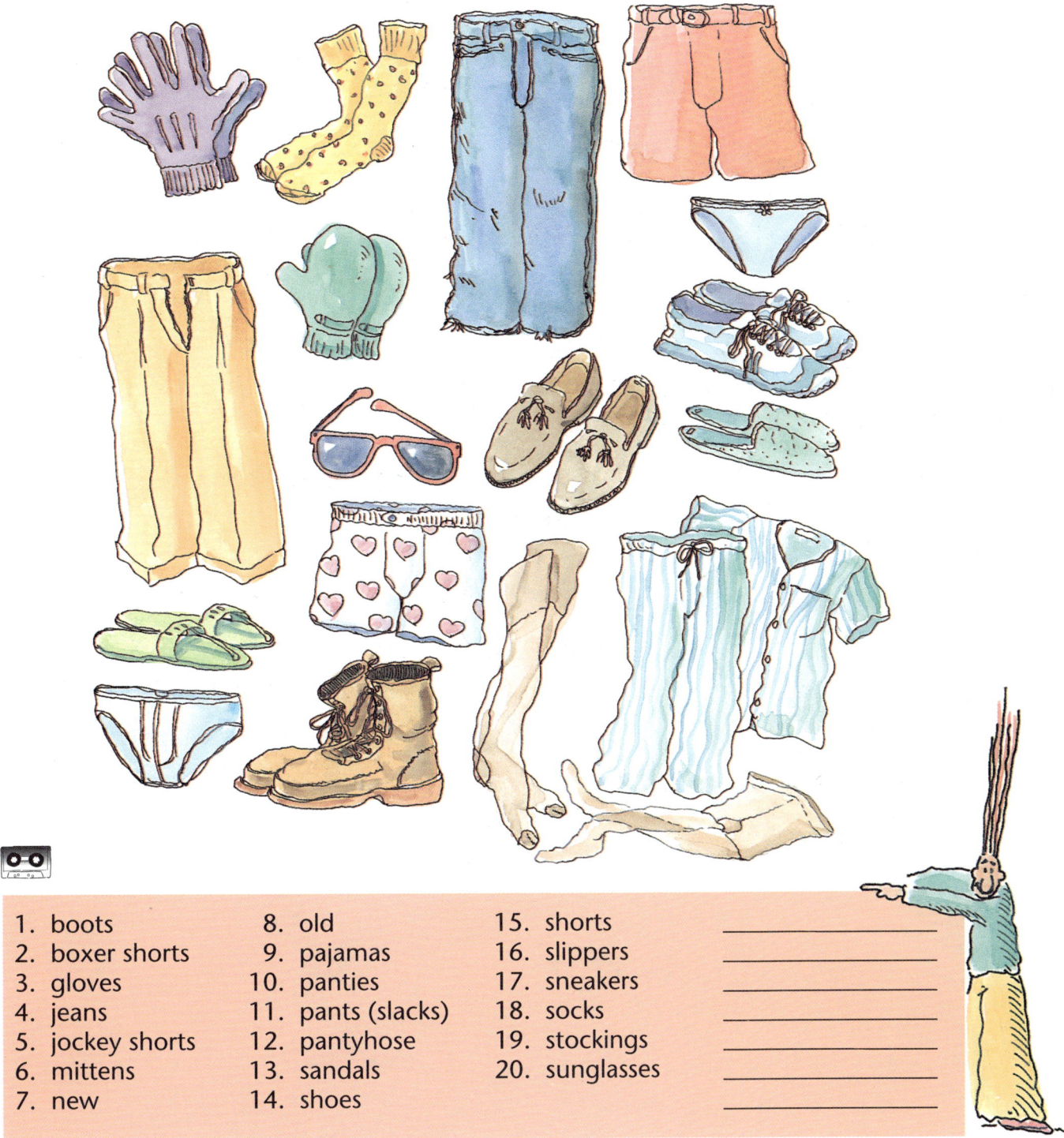

1. boots	8. old	15. shorts	_____
2. boxer shorts	9. pajamas	16. slippers	_____
3. gloves	10. panties	17. sneakers	_____
4. jeans	11. pants (slacks)	18. socks	_____
5. jockey shorts	12. pantyhose	19. stockings	_____
6. mittens	13. sandals	20. sunglasses	_____
7. new	14. shoes		_____

Group Game: *"True or false?"*

Work in groups of four. • Write three true statements about your clothes. • Write one false statement. • Read your statements to your group. • Who can guess the false statement?

Group Game: *"What am I wearing?"*

Describe the clothing of a student in another group. • Who can guess that student's name?

See Conversation Springboards on pages 94 and 95.

FAMILY

1. grandmother } grandparents
2. grandfather

3. mother } parents
4. father

5. sister-in-law
6. brother-in-law } in-laws
7. mother-in-law
8. father-in-law

9. daughter } children
10. son

11. dog } pets
12. cat

13. adult
14. child

15. wife
16. husband

17. sister } siblings
18. brother

19. aunt
20. uncle
21. niece
22. nephew

23. single parent
24. cousin

See Conversation Springboards on page 95.

Tell the Class

Can you add more words to the list? • *Tell the class about a favorite person in your family.*

1. favorite	5. nice	9. short	13. wise	_____
2. funny	6. old	10. sympathetic	14. young	_____
3. heavy	7. photo	11. tall		_____
4. helpful	8. portrait	12. thin		_____

Partner Interview   Partner's Name _____

Practice these questions with your teacher. • *Then ask your partner.*

1. Is your family big or small?
2. How many people are in your family?
3. How many brothers and sisters do you have?
4. Are they older or younger?
5. Do you have children?
6. Do you have a pet?

Draw

Work in groups of four or five. • *Draw a family portrait or a family tree.* • *Tell your group about your family.*

Tell the Class

Bring in photos of your family. • *Show your photos to the class.* • *Explain who everyone is.*

See Conversation Springboards on page 95.

REVIEW

Partner Interview

Partner's Name _____

Ask your partner.
1. What is your name?
2. What color are your eyes?
3. What color is your hair?
4. Are you tall or short?
5. Do you wear glasses?
6. Are you married?
7. How many sisters do you have?
8. How many brothers do you have?
9. Where are you from?
10. What language do you speak?

Find Someone Who

Review the vocabulary with your teacher. • *Fill in the name of someone who . . .*
1. _____ speaks three languages.
2. _____ has three names.
3. _____ is from a small family.
4. _____ is wearing jeans.
5. _____ is from a big city.
6. _____ wants to visit Disney World.

UNIT 2

EVERYDAY LIFE

The Classroom	14
Taking a Break	16
Time	18
Everyday Life	20
Morning Routine	22
Review	24

LEARNING STRATEGIES

➤ Make vocabulary cards for new words. Study the cards every day. Memorize five new words every day.

➤ Talk in English with a classmate on your break every day.

THE CLASSROOM

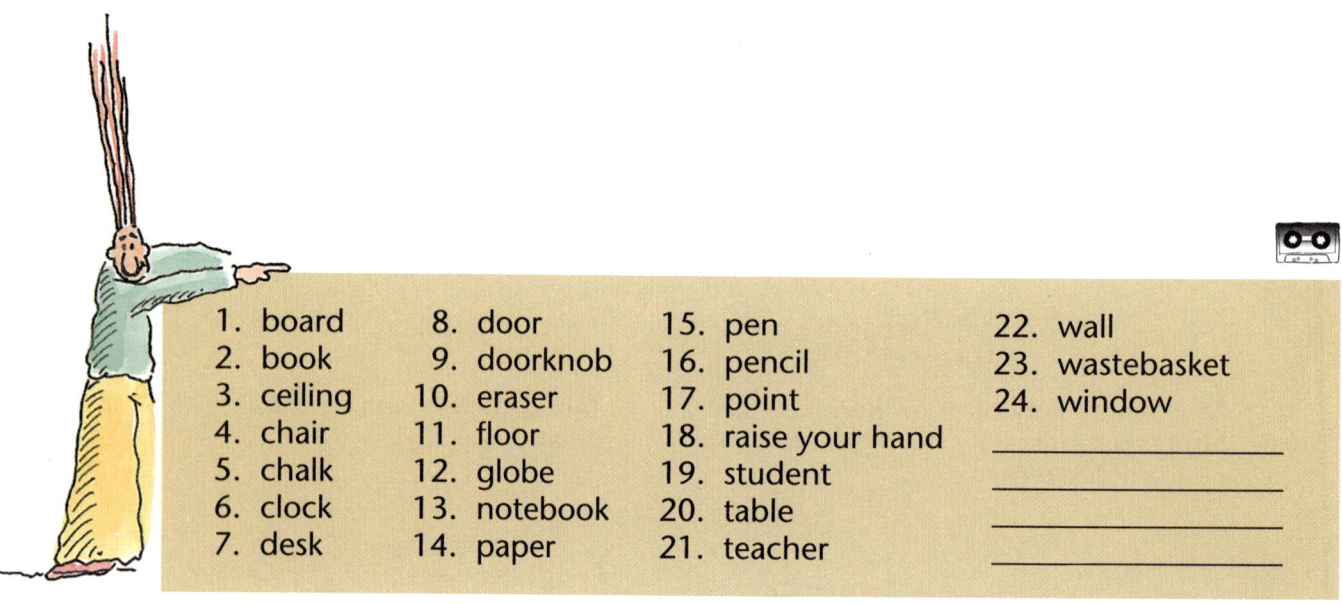

1. board
2. book
3. ceiling
4. chair
5. chalk
6. clock
7. desk
8. door
9. doorknob
10. eraser
11. floor
12. globe
13. notebook
14. paper
15. pen
16. pencil
17. point
18. raise your hand
19. student
20. table
21. teacher
22. wall
23. wastebasket
24. window

14   *See Conversation Springboards on page 95.*

Draw

Draw a picture of your classroom. • Include everything. • Work fast! • Compare pictures with other students. • Who had the most complete picture?

Group Game: "What is it?"

Work in groups of six. • Choose a leader.
     Leader: *Think about something in the classroom. Don't say it!*
     Group: *Ask the leader YES/NO questions.*
     Leader: *Answer "Yes" or "No."*
     Group: *Try to guess what it is. Whoever guesses is the new leader.*

TAKING A BREAK

1. argue	7. go out	13. sit	19. think
2. come in	8. laugh	14. sleep	20. walk
3. cry	9. listen	15. smile	21. wave
4. draw	10. look	16. speak	22. worry
5. erase	11. read	17. stand	23. write
6. frown	12. shake hands	18. talk	24. yawn

See Conversation Springboards on page 95.

Class Game: *"What am I doing?"*

Think. • *Write an activity.* • *Fold your paper.* • *Make a pile of papers.* • *Open one.* • *Follow the instruction.* • *Ask "What am I doing?"* • *Have the class guess the activity.*

Partner Game: *"How are you today?"*   Partner's Name _____

Decide how they are today. • *Write in the bubbles.* • *Fill in your own.*

1. angry
2. cold
3. happy
4. hot
5. hungry
6. nervous
7. sick
8. thirsty
9. tired

_____
_____
_____

Group Vocabulary Challenge

Work in groups of four. • *What do you do on a break?* • *Make a list with your group.* • *Read your group's list to the class.* • *With the class, make a list of the new words on the board.* • *Copy the new words into your notebook.*

See Conversation Springboards on page 95.

TIME

_____ _____ _____

_____ _____

1. afternoon	9. eat lunch	17. minute	25. wake up
2. alarm clock	10. evening	18. morning	26. watch
3. a.m.	11. get up	19. night	_____
4. clock radio	12. go to bed	20. noon	_____
5. digital clock	13. go to class	21. on time	_____
6. early	14. hour	22. p.m.	_____
7. eat breakfast	15. late	23. second	_____
8. eat dinner	16. midnight	24. study	

Class Discussion

What time is it in the pictures? • *What is the student doing?* • *Tell the picture story with your class.*

See Conversation Springboards on page 96.

Partner Interview

Partner's Name _____

Practice these questions with your teacher. • *Then ask your partner.*
1. What time do you get up in the morning?
2. What time do you eat breakfast?
3. What time do you eat lunch?
4. What time do you eat dinner?
5. How many hours is your English class?
6. How many hours do you sleep at night?

Group Survey

Ask everyone in your group these questions. • *Check YES or NO.* • *Count the answers.* • *Report your group's results to the class.* • *Write the class' results on the board.*

Do you . . .	YES	NO
1. get up early in the morning?	_____	_____
2. get up before 7:00 a.m.?	_____	_____
3. go to bed late at night?	_____	_____
4. go to bed after midnight?	_____	_____
5. have an alarm clock?	_____	_____
6. come to class on time every day?	_____	_____
7. have lunch at noon?	_____	_____

EVERYDAY LIFE

A Mother's Day

A Worker's Day

1. do homework
2. do the laundry
3. feed the baby
4. get a paycheck
5. go shopping
6. go to school
7. go to work
8. make dinner
9. punch in
10. read to the children
11. sweep the floor
12. wash the dishes
13. work

Class Discussion

Decide the correct time for each activity. • *Fill in the clocks.* • *Compare the everyday life of the mother and the worker.*

See Conversation Springboards on page 96.

Draw

Draw and write about your day.

1. _____
2. _____
3. _____
4. _____

5. _____
6. _____
7. _____
8. _____

Partner Activity

Partner's Name _____

Compare your day with your partner's day. • *What is the same?* • *What is different?*

SAME	DIFFERENT
1. _____	_____
2. _____	_____
3. _____	_____

Find Someone Who

Review the vocabulary with your teacher. • *Fill in the name of someone who . . .*

1. _____ washes the dishes every evening.
2. _____ makes dinner at home.
3. _____ punches in at work.
4. _____ does the laundry.

MORNING ROUTINE

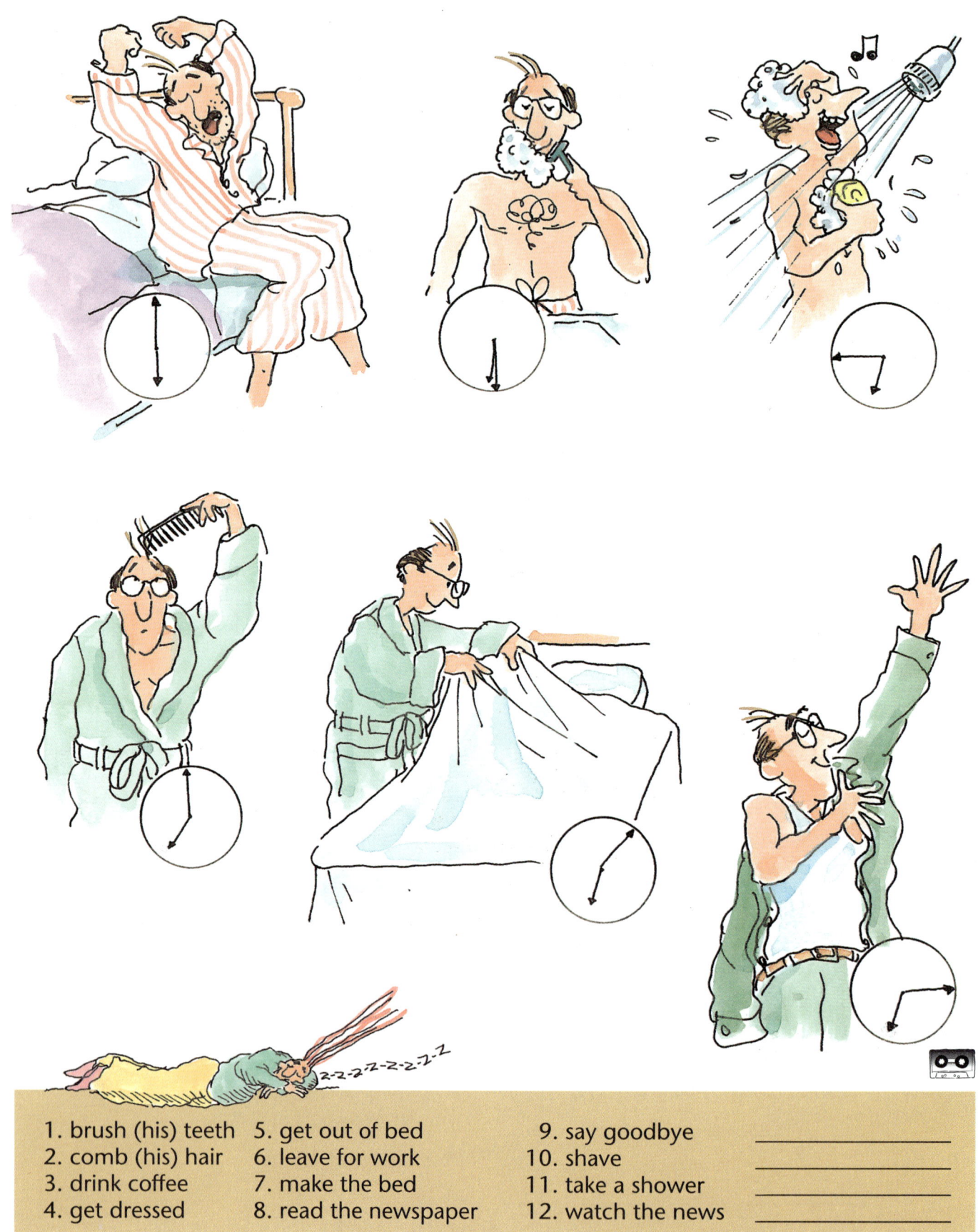

1. brush (his) teeth
2. comb (his) hair
3. drink coffee
4. get dressed
5. get out of bed
6. leave for work
7. make the bed
8. read the newspaper
9. say goodbye
10. shave
11. take a shower
12. watch the news

See Conversation Springboards on page 96.

What's the Story?

Work in groups of three. • Write a story about the man. • Everyone in the group should contribute three sentences. • Read your story to the class.

Group Game: "What do you do in the morning?"

Work in groups of five. • Pantomime a morning routine activity for your group. • No speaking! • Whoever guesses the activity takes the next turn.

REVIEW

Group Vocabulary Challenge

Work in groups of five. • Make a list of all the vocabulary from your classroom. • Compare your list with another group. • Which group had the most new words? • Make a list of the new words on the board. • Copy the new words into your notebook.

Class Activity

List ten questions about your day. • Write them on the board.

Partner Activity   Partner's Name _____

Ask your partner the questions from the Class Activity. • Present your interview to the class.

Partner Game: *"What do you do every day?"*   Partner's Name _____

Take turns. • Pantomime what you do every day. • No speaking! • Let your partner guess. • List five of the activities. • Show your class what your partner does every day.

24

UNIT 3

THE CALENDAR

Days of the Week	26
Months and Dates	28
Birthdays	30
Holidays	32
Seasons	34
Weather	36
Weather Report	38
Seasonal Clothing	39
Review	40

LEARNING STRATEGIES

➤ Make a calendar in English for this month. Write your activities on the calendar every day.

➤ In the Journal section of your notebook, write about the weather every day. For example, "Today the weather is . . ."

DAYS OF THE WEEK

	SUNDAY	MONDAY	TUESDAY	WEDNESDAY	THURSDAY	FRIDAY	SATURDAY
MORNING							
AFTERNOON							
EVENING							

1. ago
2. calendar
3. every day
4. last week
5. next week
6. sometimes
7. (the) day after tomorrow
8. (the) day before yesterday
9. this week
10. today
11. tomorrow
12. weekday
13. weekend
14. yesterday

Write

What are you doing every day this week? • *Fill in the calendar.* • *Explain it to your partner.*

See Conversation Springboards on pages 96 and 97.

Partner Interview
Partner's Name _____

Practice these questions with your teacher. • *Then ask your partner.*
1. What is today?
2. What day is tomorrow?
3. What day was yesterday? What did you do yesterday?
4. What day was the day before yesterday?
5. What are you going to do next weekend?
6. What did you do last weekend?
7. Did you come to class last week?
8. Which is your favorite day? Why?
9. What are the days of the week?

Group Survey

Ask everyone in your group these questions. • *Check YES, NO, or SOMETIMES.* • *Count the answers.* • *Report your group's results to the class.* • *Write the class' results on the board.*

Do you . . .	YES	NO	SOMETIMES
1. sleep late on Sundays?	_____	_____	_____
2. shop on Saturday afternoons?	_____	_____	_____
3. study late in the evening?	_____	_____	_____
4. go to the movies on Friday evenings?	_____	_____	_____
5. work on the weekend?	_____	_____	_____

MONTHS AND DATES

JANUARY	FEBRUARY	MARCH	APRIL
MAY	JUNE	JULY	AUGUST
SEPTEMBER	OCTOBER	NOVEMBER	DECEMBER

1st (first)
2nd (second)
3rd (third)
4th (fourth)
5th (fifth)
6th (sixth)
7th (seventh)
8th (eighth)
9th (ninth)
10th (tenth)
11th (eleventh)
12th (twelfth)
13th (thirteenth)
14th (fourteenth)
15th (fifteenth)
16th (sixteenth)
17th (seventeenth)
18th (eighteenth)
19th (nineteenth)
20th (twentieth)
21st (twenty-first)
22nd (twenty-second)
23rd (twenty-third)
24th (twenty-fourth)
25th (twenty-fifth)
26th (twenty-sixth)
27th (twenty-seventh)
28th (twenty-eighth)
29th (twenty-ninth)
30th (thirtieth)
31st (thirty-first)

century
leap year
year
_____
_____

See Conversation Springboards on page 97.

Class Discussion

1. What's today's date?
2. What was last month?
3. What is next month?
4. What date does this course end?
5. What is the date of the next holiday?
6. When is the next leap year?
7. What century is this?

Group Activity

Work in groups of five or six. • *Decide on important dates.* • *Write them on your calendars.* • *Compare your dates with the rest of the class.*

Include:
1. your birthdays (or name days)
2. other important dates
3. important holidays in your countries

Class Game: *"What is your favorite month?"*

Think. • *Write.* • *Fold your paper.* • *Make a pile of papers.* • *Open one.* • *Read it to the class.* • *Guess who wrote it.*

BIRTHDAYS

1. balloon
2. birthday cake
3. blow out the candles
4. candle
5. celebrate
6. cup
7. fork
8. gift
9. hide
10. horn
11. knife
12. make a wish
13. paper napkin
14. paper plate
15. party
16. party hat
17. present
18. punch
19. spoon
20. surprise

What's the Story?

Work in groups of four. • *Write a story about the birthday party.* • *Everyone in the group should contribute at least one sentence.* • *Read your story to the class.*

1. What kind of celebration is this?
2. Whose birthday do you think it is?
3. How old is s/he?
4. What is on the table?
5. What do you think the presents are?

See Conversation Springboards on page 97.

Partner Interview   Partner's Name _____

Practice these questions with your teacher. • Then ask your partner.
1. What do you like to give as a birthday gift to a friend? to a parent? to a co-worker? to a teacher? to a child?
2. When is your birthday? (or your name day?)
3. What kind of birthday cake is your favorite?
4. Describe how you like to celebrate your birthday (or your name day).

Write   Partner's Name _____

When is your partner's birthday? • Write a message to your partner on the card. • Sign the birthday card. • Give it to your partner. • Read your message to your partner.

Cross-Cultural Exchange

Do people celebrate birthdays or do they celebrate name days in your country? • Tell the class how they celebrate. • How do you say "Happy Birthday" in your native language? • Teach it to the class.

HOLIDAYS

Date: _____

Date: _____

Date: _____

Date: _____

1. band
2. champagne
3. chocolates
4. costume
5. decorations
6. fireworks
7. flag
8. flowers
9. ghost
10. Halloween
11. Happy Halloween!
12. Happy New Year!
13. Happy Valentine's Day!
14. I love you!
15. Independence Day
16. jack-o'-lantern
17. New Year's Eve
18. parade
19. pumpkin
20. streamers
21. Trick or Treat!
22. Valentine's Day
23. witch
_____
_____
_____
_____
_____
_____

See Conversation Springboards on page 97.

Date: _____   Date: _____

1. apple pie
2. Christmas
3. Christmas lights
4. Merry Christmas!
5. Native Americans
6. Pilgrims
7. Santa Claus
8. settlers
9. Thanksgiving
10. tree
11. turkey
_____
_____
_____

Class Activity

Fill in the dates of this year's holidays with your class. • What is your favorite holiday? • Tell the class.

Conversation Squares

Work in groups of three. • First write your own answers. • Then ask your partners the questions. • Write their answers. • Compare your group's answers with other groups.

Favorite	You _____	Partner 1 _____	Partner 2 _____
holiday	_____	_____	_____
holiday food	_____	_____	_____
holiday activity	_____	_____	_____

Cross-Cultural Exchange

How do you say "Merry Christmas" and "Happy New Year" in your native language? • Teach it to the class. • Make a list on the board. • Do you know a holiday song from your country? • Sing it for the class.

Speech

Tell the class about your favorite holiday. • Include the date, special activities, holiday food, and decorations.

See Conversation Springboards on page 97.

SEASONS

1. beach	8. farm stand	15. plow	22. summer
2. beach towel	9. garden	16. rake	23. tulip
3. bird	10. harvest	17. sled	24. volleyball
4. cider	11. ice	18. snow	25. water
5. cooler	12. ice skates	19. snowball	26. winter
6. egg	13. leaf	20. snowman	_____
7. fall (autumn)	14. nest	21. spring	_____

See Conversation Springboards on page 98.

Class Discussion

1. Where you live now, are the seasons the same as in the pictures?
2. What happens in each season?
3. What do you like to do in each season?
4. Which season is your favorite?
5. Are the seasons the same in your native city? What is different? What is the same?

What's the Story?

Work in groups of three. • *Choose one season.* • *Write a story.* • *Everyone in the group should contribute at least two sentences.* • *Read your story to the class.*

1. What are the people wearing?
2. What are they doing?
3. Do they like what they are doing?

Partner Game: *"What do you remember?"*   Partner's Name _____

Look at the picture with your partner. • *Remember as much as you can.* • *Close your book.* • *Describe the picture with your partner.* • *List everything.* • *Compare your notes with another pair.* • *Add to your list.*

WEATHER

1. bench
2. cactus
3. clear
4. cloud
5. cowboy
6. dust storm
7. grass
8. hail
9. hailstorm
10. hill
11. horse
12. lightning
13. nap
14. picnic
15. puddle
16. rain
17. saddle
18. snowstorm
19. splash
20. storm
21. sun
22. sunshine
23. thunder
24. thunderstorm
25. umbrella
26. warm
27. wet
28. wind

Class Discussion

What are the people in the pictures doing? • *What are they thinking?*

36 See Conversation Springboards on page 98.

Partner Interview

Partner's Name _____

Practice these questions with your teacher. • *Then ask your partner.*

What do you like to do . . .

1. on a rainy day?
2. on a sunny day?
3. on a cold day?
4. on a snowy day?

Find Someone Who

Review the vocabulary with your teacher. • *Fill in the name of someone who . . .*

1. _____ never saw snow.
2. _____ was in a dust storm.
3. _____ was in a thunderstorm.
4. _____ likes rain.
5. _____ likes winter.
6. _____ likes to be outside in cold weather.
7. _____ likes to be outside in hot weather.
8. _____ was hit by hail.

WEATHER REPORT

1. cloudy	8. north	15. southeast
2. cool	9. northeast	16. southwest
3. dry	10. northwest	17. sunny
4. east	11. rainy	18. temperature
5. meteorologist	12. showers	19. weather map
6. midwest	13. snowflakes	20. west
7. mild	14. south	21. windy

Group Activity

Work in groups of three. • Look at the weather map. • Report on the weather in the following areas. • Compare your answers with another group.

1. the Northeast
2. the Southeast
3. the Southwest
4. the Northwest
5. the Midwest

Community Activities

Bring in a weather report from either a native-language or an English newspaper. • Compare your report with others in the class.
Watch a weather report on TV. • Take notes:

1. What channel did you watch?
2. What time was the report on?
3. Who was the meteorologist?
4. What was the weather report for today?
5. Was it accurate?

See Conversation Springboards on page 98.

SEASONAL CLOTHING

1. bathing suit	6. long underwear	11. slicker	_____
2. bikini	7. poncho	12. stocking cap	_____
3. cutoffs	8. rubbers	13. swim trunks	_____
4. earmuffs	9. ski jacket	14. tank top	_____
5. halter	10. ski pants	15. vest	_____

Partner Interview   Partner's Name _____

Practice these questions with your teacher. • *Then ask your partner.*

1. What do you wear in cold weather?
2. What do you wear when it rains?
3. What do you wear in hot weather?
4. What do you wear when you go to the beach?
5. What do you wear when you go on a picnic?

Speech

Tell the class about the weather in your hometown. • *Use these questions as a guide:*

1. Are there seasons in your hometown? What are they? When are they?
2. What is the weather like in each season?
3. What do people wear in each season?

See Conversation Springboards on page 98.

REVIEW

Partner Interview Partner's Name _____

Practice these questions with your teacher. • *Then ask your partner.*

1. What is today's date?
2. What's the weather like today?
3. Is it hot? cold? warm? cool?
4. What season is it?
5. Do you like this weather?
6. What do you want to do today?

Write

Write in your journal.

Journal

_____ (1)

Today is a _____ day. It is
                  (2)

_____ during this season of _____.
   (3)   (4)

I _____ the weather
         (5)

today. It is a good day to _____.
                                  (6)

Tell Your Partner

Read your journal entry to your partner. • *Listen to your partner's journal.*

UNIT 4

FOOD

Fruit	42
Vegetables	44
Meat, Seafood, and Poultry	46
Desserts	48
Breakfast	50
Lunch	52
Fast Food	54
Junk Food	56
Dinner	57
The Supermarket	58
Review	60

LEARNING STRATEGIES

➤ Have lunch with one or more friends. Speak only English at lunch.

➤ Find food labels in English. Read the labels out loud. Ask your teacher about the pronunciation of new words.

FRUIT

1. apple	8. buy	15. lemon	22. pineapple	29. strawberry
2. apricot	9. cantaloupe	16. lime	23. pit	30. watermelon
3. banana	10. cherry	17. mango	24. plum	
4. blackberry	11. coconut	18. orange	25. pound	
5. blueberry	12. grape	19. papaya	26. raspberry	
6. box	13. grapefruit	20. peach	27. seeds	
7. bunch	14. kiwi	21. pear	28. skin	

See Conversation Springboards on pages 98 and 99.

Partner Interview

Partner's Name _____

Practice these questions with your teacher. • *Then ask your partner.*

1. What is your favorite kind of fruit?
2. What other fruit do you like?
3. What fruit grows in your country?
4. What fruit can you buy in your neighborhood?

Group Game: *"Preparing fruit salad"*

Work in groups of four. • *Prepare a fruit salad for the next class.*

To Get Ready:

What kind of fruit will each student bring?

_____ _____

_____ _____

Who will bring a bowl? _____
Who will bring a knife? _____
Who will bring a large spoon? _____
Who will bring a fork? _____

To Demonstrate:

- *Prepare your fruit salad.*

- *Compare the fruit salads.*

- *Vote on the best one.*

- *Enjoy the snack!*

VEGETABLES

1. artichoke	6. carrot	11. fresh	16. peas	
2. bean	7. celery	12. head	17. pepper	
3. beet	8. corn	13. lettuce	18. potato	
4. broccoli	9. cucumber	14. mushroom	19. produce	
5. cabbage	10. ear	15. onion	20. tomato	

See Conversation Springboards on page 99.

Partner Interview

Partner's Name _____

Practice these questions with your teacher. • *Then ask your partner.*

1. What is your favorite vegetable?
2. What vegetables don't you like?
3. What vegetables grow in your country?
4. Which vegetables do you usually use for salad?
5. What do fresh vegetables usually cost at your market?
6. Which vegetables do you buy by the bunch? by the head? by the ear? by the pound?

Group Decision

Work in groups of five or six. • *Decide which vegetables to use for a salad.* • *Decide how to prepare each vegetable.* • *Tell the class about your salad.*

VEGETABLE	YES/NO	COOKED	RAW	PEELED	SLICED	SHREDDED
carrots	_____	_____	_____	_____	_____	_____
tomatoes	_____	_____	_____	_____	_____	_____
celery	_____	_____	_____	_____	_____	_____
lettuce	_____	_____	_____	_____	_____	_____
onions	_____	_____	_____	_____	_____	_____
green beans	_____	_____	_____	_____	_____	_____
mushrooms	_____	_____	_____	_____	_____	_____
peppers	_____	_____	_____	_____	_____	_____
other	_____	_____	_____	_____	_____	_____
TOTALS	_____	_____	_____	_____	_____	_____

MEAT, SEAFOOD, AND POULTRY

1. can	7. hot dogs	13. meatballs	19. sausages	
2. chicken	8. lamb chops	14. octopus	20. shrimp	
3. crab meat	9. lamb roast	15. package	21. steak	25. tuna fish
4. fish	10. leg of lamb	16. pig's feet	22. stew beef	_____
5. ground beef	11. liver	17. pork chops	23. swordfish	_____
6. ham	12. lobster	18. roast beef	24. tuna	_____

Partner Interview   **Partner's Name** _____

Practice these questions with your teacher. • *Then ask your partner.*

1. Do you eat meat? What is your favorite meat?
2. Do you eat poultry? What is your favorite?
3. Do you eat seafood? What is your favorite fish? What is your favorite shellfish?
4. Which meats, fish, and poultry are most common in your country?
5. Are there any meats, fish, or poultry that you never eat? Why?
6. Where do you buy meats? fish? poultry?
7. Is it a good idea to eat a lot of red meat? Why? Why not?

See Conversation Springboards on page 99.

1. bake   4. broil   7. roast   10. steam   _____
2. barbecue 5. casserole 8. seasoning 11. stir fry _____
3. boil   6. fry   9. simmer   _____

Find Someone Who

How do you like your food prepared? • *Review the vocabulary with your teacher.* • *Fill in the name of someone who . . .*

1. _____ likes baked fish with salt and pepper.
2. _____ prepares barbecued spare ribs.
3. _____ doesn't eat fried food.
4. _____ knows how to prepare stir fry.
5. _____ likes meat simmered in sauce.
6. _____ likes casseroles.
7. _____ likes food with chili powder.
8. _____ broils steak with seasoning.

See Conversation Springboards on page 99.

DESSERTS

1. beverage	7. coffee	13. frozen yogurt	19. milkshake	25. tea
2. brownie	8. coffeecake	14. ice cream	20. pastry	_____
3. cake	9. cone	15. ice cream soda	21. pie	_____
4. candy	10. cookies	16. iced coffee	22. pie a la mode	_____
5. cappuccino	11. doughnut	17. iced tea	23. sherbet	_____
6. cheesecake	12. espresso	18. lemonade	24. sundae	_____

What's the Story?

Work in groups of five. • Choose one table. • Write a story about the people. • Everyone in the group should contribute at least two sentences. • Read your story to the class.

1. Who are the people?
2. Where are they?
3. What are they eating?
4. What are the children's favorite desserts?
5. What are the adults' favorite desserts?

See Conversation Springboards on page 99.

Group Discussion

Work in groups of five. • *Discuss these questions.* • *Report your answers to the class.*

1. What is your favorite dessert?
2. Do you buy it or prepare it?
3. How do you prepare it?
4. Is it fattening?
5. How often do you have your favorite dessert?

Group Role Play

Work in groups of five. • *First fill in this menu with the desserts your group likes.* • *Decide on prices.* • *Then write a role play ordering dessert and coffee (or tea) at a coffee shop.* • *Present your role play to the class.*

Cross-Cultural Exchange

Bring your favorite desserts or pastries to class. • *Take a break.* • *Have a dessert party.* • *Taste everyone's dessert!*

BREAKFAST

1. bacon	7. cream	13. home fries	19. oatmeal
2. bagel	8. cream cheese	14. jam	20. orange juice
3. butter	9. Danish	15. jelly	21. pancakes
4. cereal	10. French toast	16. margarine	22. sugar
5. cereal bowl	11. (fried) egg	17. milk	23. syrup
6. cocoa	12. grits	18. muffin	24. toast

Partner Interview Partner's Name _____

Practice these questions with your teacher. • *Then ask your partner.*

1. What is a typical breakfast for you?
2. What time do you eat breakfast?
3. Do you eat breakfast with your family?
4. Do you eat breakfast at home?
5. In your opinion, what is a healthy breakfast?

See Conversation Springboards on page 100.

Cross-Cultural Exchange

What do people usually eat for breakfast in your country? • *Tell the class.* • *Add new vocabulary to the list.*

Conversation Squares

Work in groups of three. • *First write your own answers.* • *Then ask your partners the questions.* • *Write their answers.* • *Compare your group's answers with other groups.*

Breakfast	You	Partner 1	Partner 2
today	_____	_____	_____
yesterday	_____	_____	_____
tomorrow	_____	_____	_____

Group Survey

Ask everyone in your group these questions. • *Check ALWAYS, SOMETIMES, or NEVER.* • *Count the answers.* • *Report your group's results to the class.* • *Write the class' results on the board.*

How often do you . . .	ALWAYS	SOMETIMES	NEVER
1. skip breakfast?	_____	_____	_____
2. drink coffee for breakfast?	_____	_____	_____
3. have cold cereal for breakfast?	_____	_____	_____
4. have hot cereal for breakfast?	_____	_____	_____
5. have fruit or juice for breakfast?	_____	_____	_____
6. have something sweet for breakfast?	_____	_____	_____
7. eat out for breakfast?	_____	_____	_____
8. eat a nutritious breakfast?	_____	_____	_____

LUNCH

1. boiled ham	12. ketchup	23. roll	27. slice of bread
2. bologna	13. leftovers	24. salad	28. soup
3. bread	14. lunch box	25. salami	29. spaghetti
4. brown paper bag/sack	15. lunchroom	26. sandwich	30. spaghetti sauce
5. cafeteria	16. mayonnaise		31. thermos
6. cheese	17. microwave oven		32. yogurt
7. coffee mug	18. mustard		
8. cold cuts	19. peanut butter		
9. frozen entree	20. plastic baggie		
10. ham sandwich	21. potato chips		
11. hero (submarine/grinder)	22. roast beef sandwich		

What's the Story?

Work in groups of five. • *Choose one scene and write a story.* • *Everyone in the group should contribute at least two sentences.* • *Read your story to the class.*

1. Where are the people?
2. What are their names?
3. What are they eating and drinking?
4. What are they saying?

See Conversation Springboards on page 100.

Partner Interview

Partner's Name _____

Practice these questions with your teacher. • *Then ask your partner.*

1. What time do you usually eat lunch?
2. Where do you eat lunch?
3. What do you usually eat for lunch?
4. What do you usually drink for lunch?
5. Do you usually eat a nutritious lunch?
6. Do you ever skip lunch? Why?
7. Do you bring your lunch to work? to school? What do you bring?
8. Do you make your own lunch? If not, who makes it for you?
9. If you buy your lunch, where do you buy it? How much does it cost?
10. Who do you usually eat lunch with? What do you talk about?

Write

What is your favorite sandwich? • *How do you prepare it?* • *Write the recipe.* • *Tell the class how to make your favorite sandwich.*

Recipe

_____
(1)

Spread _____ on
(2)

_____ .
(3)

Put _____ on the bread
(4)

and close the sandwich.

Cut in half.
Enjoy the sandwich!

Choose one:

(1) roast beef sandwich
     peanut butter & jelly
     tuna fish sandwich
     ham & cheese sandwich
     other:_____

(2) mayonnaise
     butter
     margarine
     mustard
     ketchup
     peanut butter
     other:_____

(3) rye bread
     white bread
     wheat bread
     a roll
     other:_____

(4) roast beef
     tuna fish
     ham and cheese
     jelly
     other:_____

FAST FOOD

1. bun
2. cashier
3. cash register
4. change
5. chicken nuggets
6. counter
7. customer
8. drive-in/drive-thru window
9. hamburger
10. hot sauce (salsa)
11. line
12. order
13. pay
14. pickle
15. salad bar
16. salad dressing
17. shake
18. soft drink
19. straw

See Conversation Springboards on page 100.

Group Survey

Ask everyone in your group these questions. • Check YES or NO. • Count the answers. • Report your group's results to the class. • Write the class' results on the board.

Do you . . .	YES	NO
1. ever eat fast foods?	_____	_____
2. like hamburgers with "everything"?	_____	_____
3. like French fries?	_____	_____
4. like ketchup on your fries?	_____	_____
5. like chicken nuggets?	_____	_____
6. like hot dogs?	_____	_____
7. like mustard on your hot dogs?	_____	_____
8. like soft drinks?	_____	_____
9. like salsa?	_____	_____
10. think fast food is bad for you?	_____	_____

Partner Role Play

With your partner, complete this role play. • Present your role play to the class.

Cashier: May I help you?
Customer: _____

Cashier: Anything to drink?
Customer: _____

Cashier: Anything else?
Customer: _____

Cashier: That'll be $ _____.__, please.

Customer: Here's _____
   [Customer gives cashier $20.00.]

Cashier: That's $_____ change. Have a nice day.
   [Cashier takes out change from the cash register, and gives change to customer.]

JUNK FOOD

1. bubble gum	6. crackers	11. pretzels
2. candy bar	7. gum	12. snack machine
3. cheese snack	8. juice drink	13. soda
4. chocolate bar	9. peanuts	14. tortilla chips
5. corn chips	10. popcorn	15. vending machine

Class Discussion

1. Which junk foods do you like? Which don't you like?
2. Do you ever eat junk food? When?
3. Where do you buy junk food?

Class Game: "What is your favorite junk food?"

Write the name of your favorite junk food. • Fold your paper. • Make a pile. • Open one. • Guess who wrote it. • Who likes the same junk food?

Group Decision

Work in groups of five or six. • Your group has $5.00 to spend on snacks. • Look at the picture. • What will you buy from the snack machines? • Tell the class.

See Conversation Springboards on page 100.

DINNER

1. ash tray
2. beer
3. busboy
4. check
5. glass of water
6. hostess
7. maitre d'
8. nonsmoking section
9. restaurant
10. restroom
11. smoking section
12. tip
13. waiter
14. waitress
15. wine

What's the Story?

Work in groups of five. • Write a story about one of the tables in the picture. • Everyone in the group should contribute at least one sentence. • Read your story to the class.

1. Who are the people? What are their names?
2. Why are they going out to eat tonight?
3. What are they having for dinner?
4. How are they feeling tonight?
5. What are they saying?
6. Who will pay the check?
7. What will they do after they leave the restaurant?

See Conversation Springboards on pages 100 and 101.

THE SUPERMARKET

1. aisle
2. bottle
3. bottle return
4. can return
5. carton
6. checkout counter
7. courtesy desk
8. dozen
9. grated cheese
10. jar
11. loaf
12. rice
13. section
14. shelf
15. shopping cart
16. tomato paste
17. whipped cream
_____
_____
_____

Group Vocabulary Challenge

Work in groups of four. • List as many supermarket items as you can. • Compare your list with another group.

Group Decision

Work in groups of three or four. • Compare these jars of tomato sauce. • Tell the class about your findings.

 32 oz. $2.19

 24 oz. $1.49

 8 oz. $.59

largest
smallest
most expensive
cheapest
best buy

See Conversation Springboards on page 101.

Community Activity

Review this list with your teacher. • Add two items. • Go to your supermarket. • Fill out the chart. • In the next class, compare your charts.

Supermarket Name: _____

ITEM	SIZE	BRAND NAME	PRICE
1. bread	_____	_____	_____
2. coffee	_____	_____	_____
3. rice	_____	_____	_____
4. _____	_____	_____	_____
5. _____	_____	_____	_____

REVIEW

Group Decision

Work in groups of five or six. • Choose one of the family pictures. • Plan menus for one day (breakfast, lunch, dinner, and snacks) for the family. • Figure the cost.

Breakfast

_____
_____ $_____
_____
_____

Lunch

_____
_____
_____ $_____
_____
_____

Dinner

_____
_____ $_____
_____
_____

Snacks

_____
_____
_____ $_____
_____
_____

Class Game: "What is it?"

Choose a leader.

    Leader: Think of a food you like. Don't say it!
    Class: Ask the leader YES/NO questions.
    Leader: Answer "Yes" or "No."
    Class: Try to guess the food. Whoever guesses is the new leader.

Cross-Cultural Exchange

Bring special foods from your country to class. • Have an international party. • Bring music from your country to play at the party. • Enjoy!

UNIT 5

HOMES

City or Country	62
Homes	64
The Kitchen	66
The Dining Room	68
The Living Room	70
The Bedroom	72
The Bathroom	74
At Home	75
Neighbors	76
Problems at Home	78
Review	80

LEARNING STRATEGIES

➤ Make labels in English for everything in your home. Repeat the new vocabulary every time you look at a label.

➤ With a classmate, describe each room in your home. Then compare your homes.

CITY OR COUNTRY

1. beautiful
2. busy
3. calm
4. coast
5. crowded
6. desert
7. exciting
8. farm
9. grow up
10. jungle
11. live
12. mountain
13. noisy
14. peaceful
15. ranch
16. rural
17. suburban
_____
_____
_____

Partner Interview

Partner's Name _____

Practice these questions with your teacher. • *Then ask your partner.*

1. Where do you live now?
2. How long have you lived there?
3. Where were you born?
4. Where did you grow up?
5. Where do you want to live?

See Conversation Springboards on page 101.

Group Discussion

Work in groups of three. • *Discuss these questions.* • *Report your answers to the class.*
1. Do you like where you live now?
2. In your opinion, where is the best place in the world to live?
3. Decide as a group which place you like best. Tell your class why. If you can't agree on a place, tell your class why you can't agree.

Speech

Bring in a picture or a photo of a beautiful place to live. • *Tell the class about the picture.* • *Use these questions as a guide.*
1. Where is the place?
2. Why do you think it is beautiful?
3. Why do you want to live there?

Group Game: "Gossip!"

Work in groups of eight. • *Choose a leader.* • *Close your books.* • *Look at the cover.* • *What are the people saying?*

Leader: [*To the first student*] Read the secret on page 125. Close your book. Whisper the secret to the student sitting next to you.
That Student: [*Whisper the secret to the student sitting next to you, etc.*]
Last Student: [*Write the secret on the board or tell the class.*]
Class: [*Check the secret on page 125. Which group had the most accurate secret?*]

HOMES

1. apartment (flat)
2. attic
3. awning
4. balcony
5. basement
6. brick
7. cactus garden
8. cement
9. chimney
10. condominium
11. dormitory
12. fence
13. garage
14. house
15. mobile home
16. porch
17. prison
18. private home
19. roof
20. steps
21. stucco
22. terrace
23. wood
24. yard

What's the Story?

Work in groups of three. • Decide which home to describe. • Write a story about the home and the people. • Everyone in the group should contribute at least two sentences. • Read your story to the class.

See Conversation Springboards on pages 101 and 102.

Conversation Squares

Work in groups of four. • First write your own answers. • Then ask your partners the questions. • Write their answers. • Compare your group's answers with other groups. • Make a class directory.

1. What's your name? First/Middle/Last: _____ **What's your address?** Number/Street _____ Apartment number _____ City or Town _____ State _____ ZIP Code _____ **What's your phone number?** Area Code: (_____) Number: _____	**3. What's your name?** First/Middle/Last: _____ **What's your address?** Number/Street _____ Apartment number _____ City or Town _____ State _____ ZIP Code _____ **What's your phone number?** Area Code: (_____) Number: _____
2. What's your name? First/Middle/Last: _____ **What's your address?** Number/Street _____ Apartment number _____ City or Town _____ State _____ ZIP Code _____ **What's your phone number?** Area Code: (_____) Number: _____	**4. What's your name?** First/Middle/Last: _____ **What's your address?** Number/Street _____ Apartment number _____ City or Town _____ State _____ ZIP Code _____ **What's your phone number?** Area Code: (_____) Number: _____

THE KITCHEN

1. burner
2. cabinet
3. can opener
4. coffee maker
5. creamer
6. cupboard
7. dishpan
8. dishwasher
9. dryer
10. electric mixer
11. faucet
12. freezer
13. frying pan
14. linoleum
15. oven
16. pot
17. refrigerator
18. sink
19. small appliance
20. stove
21. sugar bowl
22. tea kettle
23. toaster
24. washing machine
25. wok

See Conversation Springboards on page 102.

What's the Story?

Work in groups of five. • *Write a story about the kitchen.* • *Everyone in the group should contribute at least two sentences.* • *Read your story to the class.*

1. Where is the family?
2. What are their names?
3. What time is it?
4. What is the family doing?

Partner Game: *"Same or Different?"*   Partner's Name _____

One partner looks at the picture on this page. • *The other partner looks at the picture on page 66.* • *Compare kitchens.* • *List everything in both kitchens.* • *What is the same?* • *What is different?*

SAME	DIFFERENT
1. _____	_____
2. _____	_____
3. _____	_____

67

THE DINING ROOM

1. candlestick
2. glass
3. napkin
4. pepper shaker
5. pie server
6. pitcher
7. plate
8. salad bowl
9. salt shaker
10. saucer
11. serving spoon
12. set the table
13. silverware
14. soup bowl
15. tablecloth
16. tablespoon
17. teaspoon
18. vase

_____
_____
_____
_____
_____
_____

68

See Conversation Springboards on page 102.

Partner Interview

Partner's Name _____

Practice these questions with your teacher. • *Then ask your partner.*

1. What room do you eat in at home?
2. How do you set the table at home? for breakfast? lunch? dinner?
3. Does your family always eat together?

Group Activity

Work in groups of four or five. • *With your group, list five things people say at the dinner table.* • *Read your list to the class.* • *Make a list on the board.*

Group Role Play

Work in groups of five. • *Choose one scene.* • *Write a role play with your group.* • *Include roles for everyone.* • *Present your role play to the class.*

1. a family eating together
2. a family setting the table for dinner with guests
3. a teenager eating with his or her friends in the kitchen

Include in your role play:

1. the people (Give them names!)
2. how they feel
3. what they are saying
4. what is on the table
5. the food

Cross-Cultural Exchange

What are some traditional eating customs in your country? • *Tell the class.* • *How are the customs the same in different countries?* • *Which countries are the most similar?*

THE LIVING ROOM

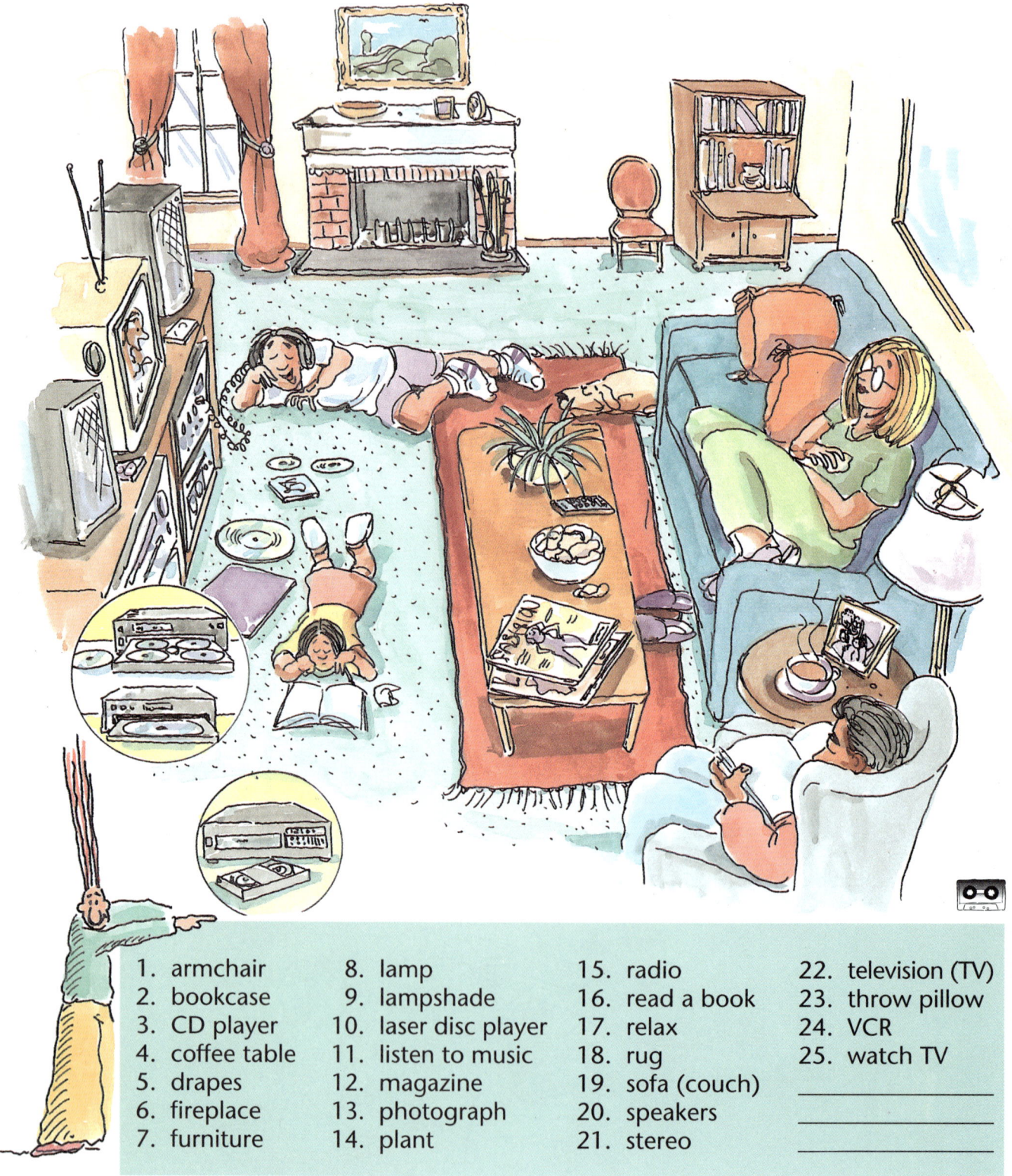

1. armchair
2. bookcase
3. CD player
4. coffee table
5. drapes
6. fireplace
7. furniture
8. lamp
9. lampshade
10. laser disc player
11. listen to music
12. magazine
13. photograph
14. plant
15. radio
16. read a book
17. relax
18. rug
19. sofa (couch)
20. speakers
21. stereo
22. television (TV)
23. throw pillow
24. VCR
25. watch TV
_____
_____
_____

Group Vocabulary Challenge

Work in groups of four. • Make a list of everything you do in your living rooms. • Read your list to the class. • Which group had the most new words? • Make a list on the board. • Copy the new words into your notebook.

See Conversation Springboards on pages 102 and 103.

Class Game: *"What do you do in the living room?"*

Think. • *Write an activity.* • *Fold your paper.* • *Make a pile of papers.* • *Open one.* • *Follow the instruction.* • *Ask "What am I doing?"* • *Have the class guess the activity.*

Group Game: *"Gossip!"*

Work in groups of eight. • *Choose a leader.* • *Close your books.* • *Look at the cover.* • *What are the people saying?*

      Leader: [To the first student] Read the secret on page 125. Close your book. Whisper the secret to the student sitting next to you.

That Student: [Whisper the secret to the student sitting next to you, etc.]

Last Student: [Write the secret on the board or tell the class.]

       Class: [Check the secret on page 125. Which group had the most accurate secret?]

Community Activity

Bring in ads from stores that sell furniture. • *Decide as a class how to furnish a living room.* • *What will you buy?* • *How much will each item cost?* • *What will the total bill be?*

bill

THE BEDROOM

1. bedspread
2. blanket
3. box spring
4. brush
5. carpet
6. chest of drawers
7. closet
8. comb
9. curtains
10. drawer
11. dresser
12. mattress
13. mirror
14. night stand
15. pillow
16. pillowcase
17. shade
18. sheets
19. telephone
20. vanity

See Conversation Springboards on page 103.

Class Game: *"What do you remember?"*

Look at the picture. • *Remember as much as you can.* • *Close your book.* • *List everything.* • *Compare your answers with the class.* • *Who had the longest list?* • *Open your book and check your answers.*

Partner Interview   Partner's Name _____

Practice these questions with your teacher. • *Then ask your partner.*

Do you remember your childhood bedroom?

1. How many windows did it have?
2. How many doors did it have?
3. What furniture was in the room?
4. Where did you keep your clothes?
5. What toys did you have in your bedroom?
6. What was on the walls?
7. What was on the floor?
8. What did you see from the window?
9. Did you like your bedroom? Why or why not?

Draw

Draw a picture of your childhood bedroom. • *Explain your picture to your partner.*

THE BATHROOM

1. aspirin
2. bandaid
3. bath towel
4. bath toy
5. bathtub
6. bubble bath
7. conditioner
8. deodorant
9. drain
10. electric razor
11. hand towel
12. mat
13. medicine cabinet
14. razor
15. shampoo
16. shaving cream
17. shower
18. shower curtain
19. soap
20. soap dish
21. tiles
22. toilet
23. toilet paper
24. toilet seat
25. toothbrush
26. toothpaste
27. towel

What's the Story?

Work in groups of three. • Write a story about the bathroom. • Everyone in the group should contribute at least three sentences. • Read your story to the class.

1. What time of day is it?
2. Who are the people?
3. What are their names?
4. What are they doing?
5. What are they going to do?
6. What are they thinking?

Cross-Cultural Exchange

Are baths or showers more popular in your country? • Is the toilet in the same room as the bath? • Do children use training toilets? • Do people sing in the shower? the bath?

See Conversation Springboards on page 103.

AT HOME

Class Vocabulary Challenge

Look at the picture. • What do you see in this home? • Make a list of the vocabulary words you can remember. • Read your list to the class. • Who has the most new words? • Make a list on the board. • Copy the new words into your notebook.

Group Survey

Ask everyone in your group these questions. • Check EVERY DAY, SOMETIMES, or NEVER. • Count the answers. • Report your group's results to the class. • Write the class' results on the board.

How often do you . . .	EVERY DAY	SOMETIMES	NEVER
1. eat lunch at home?	_____	_____	_____
2. watch TV in the evening?	_____	_____	_____
3. read magazines in the bathtub?	_____	_____	_____
4. write letters in the kitchen?	_____	_____	_____
5. talk on the telephone?	_____	_____	_____
6. take care of children?	_____	_____	_____
7. sing in the shower?	_____	_____	_____
8. cook your own meals?	_____	_____	_____
9. sleep well at night?	_____	_____	_____

See Conversation Springboards on page 103.

NEIGHBORS

1. baby-sit
2. borrow
3. bother
4. chat
5. fight
6. friendly
7. gossip
8. have a party
9. help
10. lend
11. next door
12. problem
13. secret
14. unfriendly
15. whisper

See Conversation Springboards on page 103.

Partner Interview

Partner's Name _____

Practice these questions with your teacher. • *Then ask your partner.*

1. How many neighbors do you know?
2. Are your neighbors friendly?
3. What languages do your neighbors speak?
4. Do you visit your neighbors?
5. Do the children in your neighborhood play together? What games do they play?
6. Do the children ever fight?
7. Do you have any problems with your neighbors? What kind of problems?

Group Role Play

Work in groups of four or five. • *Choose one scene.* • *Write a role play with your group.* • *Include roles for everyone.* • *Present your role play to the class.*

PROBLEMS AT HOME

1. cockroach
2. drip
3. exterminator
4. flooded
5. freezing
6. leak
7. leaking roof
8. mouse
9. (no) heat
10. off
11. on
12. overflow
13. pest
14. pesticide
15. plugged up/ stopped up
16. plunger
17. radiator
18. shiver

See Conversation Springboards on page 104.

Group Problem Posing/Problem Solving

Work in groups of five. • State the problems. • Give advice to the people. • Suggest solutions. • Read your problems and solutions to the class.

Group Role Play

Work in groups of five. • Choose one scene. • Write a role play with your group. • Include roles for everyone. • Present your role play to the class.

Strip Stories

Discuss these stories with your class. • State the problems. • What mistakes are they making? • Write captions.

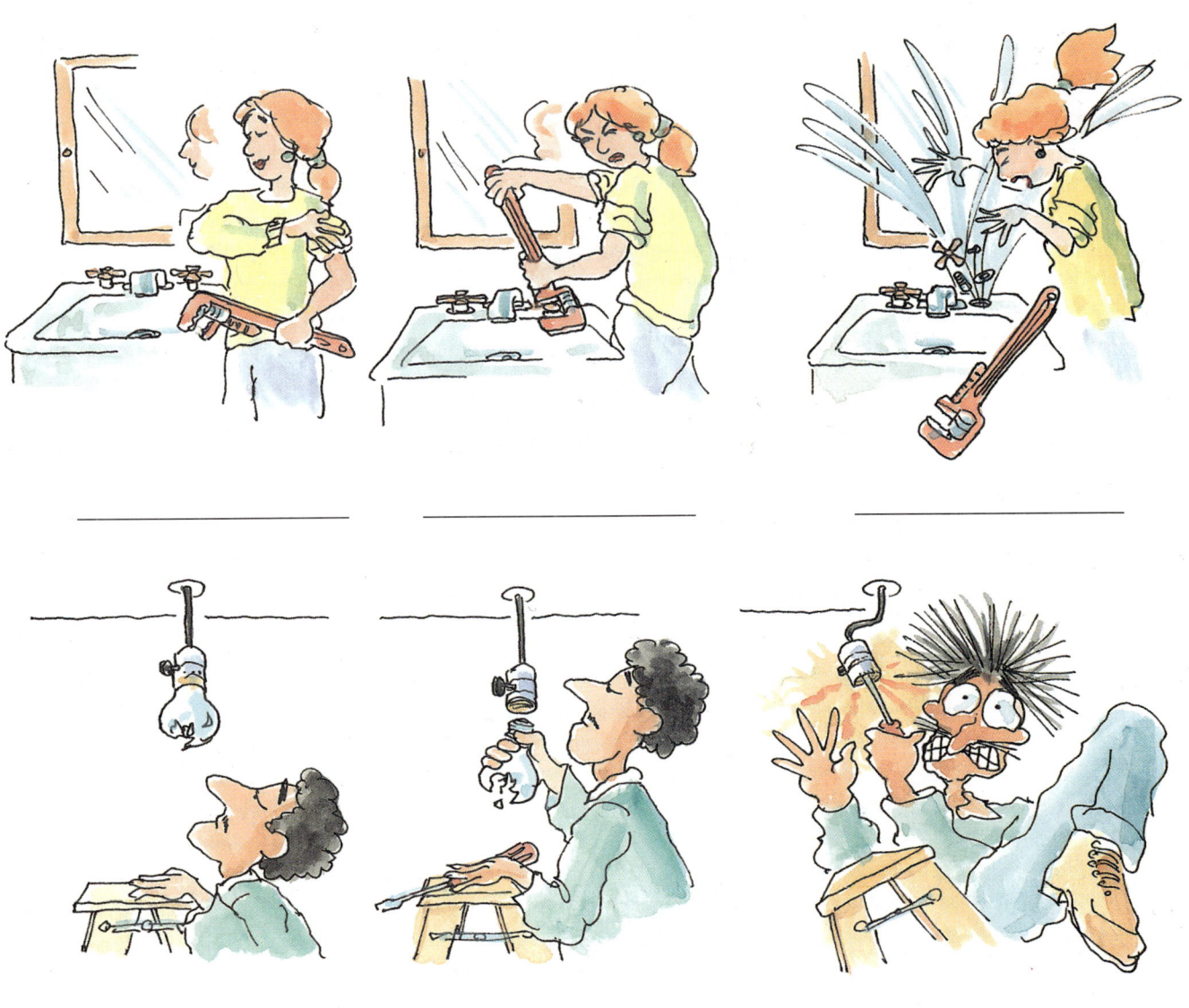

Group Activity

Work in groups of five. • Make a list of problems you have at home. • Read your list to the class. • Compare lists. • What is the biggest problem? • Make a list on the board. • Copy the new words into your notebook. • Discuss solutions for all the problems.

REVIEW

Partner Interview Partner's Name _____

Practice these questions with your teacher. • *Then ask your partner.*

1. What is today's date?
2. What is your name?
3. Where do you live?
4. How many rooms are in your home?
5. Where do you study?
6. Where do you watch TV?
7. Where do you eat breakfast?
8. Do you know your neighbors?
9. Do you like your neighbors?
10. Why?

Write

Write about your partner.

Journal

_____
(1)

My partner's name is _____. My
(2)

partner lives in _____. S/he
(3)

has _____ rooms in his/her home. S/he
(4)

studies in the _____.
(5)

S/he watches TV in the _____.
(6)

S/he eats breakfast in the _____.
(7)

S/he _____ his/her neighbors.
(8)

S/he _____ the neighbors because
(9)

_____.
(10)

Tell the Class

Read your journal to the class. • *Tell the class about your partner.*

UNIT 6

SHOPPING

Going Shopping!	82
Sporting Goods Store	84
Toy Store	86
Shoe Store	88
Men's Clothing Store	90
Women's Clothing Store	91
Review	92

LEARNING STRATEGIES

▶ Write all your shopping lists in English. Go shopping with a friend from class. Shop in English.

▶ Show your purchases to classmates. Describe your purchases in English. Ask questions about what your classmates bought.

GOING SHOPPING!

1. coffee shop (cafe)
2. department store
3. electronics store
4. flower stand
5. hardware store
6. jewelry store
7. mall
8. men's clothing store
9. music store
10. pharmacy
11. shoe store
12. shopping center
13. sporting goods store
14. stationery store
15. toy store
16. women's clothing store

See Conversation Springboards on page 104.

Class Activity

Are these stores in your neighborhood? • Write the names of your neighborhood stores on the signs. • What do you buy in each of the stores? • Make a list on the board of three items for each store.

Group Discussion

Work in groups of five. • Discuss these questions. • Report your answers to the class.

1. Where do you shop?
2. When do you go shopping?
3. What stores do you go to?
4. Which stores in your neighborhood do you like best? Why?
5. Which store do you recommend to the class?

SPORTING GOODS STORE

1. athletic equipment
2. baseball
3. baseball bat
4. baseball cap
5. baseball glove
6. basketball
7. bowling ball
8. cleats
9. fishing reel
10. fishing rod
11. flies
12. football
13. golf bag
14. golf ball
15. golf club
16. golf tee
17. helmet
18. hockey puck
19. hockey skates
20. hockey stick
21. shoulder pads
22. skates
23. ski boots
24. ski poles
25. skis
26. soccer ball
27. soccer shoes
28. sweatsuit

Class Discussion

1. What is your favorite sport?
2. Where do you buy athletic equipment?
3. What do you buy?
4. Is it expensive? How much does it cost?
5. What kind of clothing do you buy in a sporting goods store?

84   See Conversation Springboards on page 104.

Group Decision

Work in groups of four. • Decide what to buy for one of the following situations. • Report your decisions to the class.

1. Your ten-year-old nephew is having a birthday. He is on a baseball team for the first time.
2. Your sister and brother-in-law are having an anniversary. Your sister likes to play golf. Your brother-in-law likes to bowl.
3. You live in a warm climate. You want to take up a new sport.

Group Vocabulary Challenge

Work in groups of four. • Make a list of special equipment you need for these sports. • Read your list to the class. • Which group had the most new words? • Make a list on the board. • Copy the list into your notebook.

skiing	baseball
golf	hockey
ice skating	basketball
bowling	other: _____

Find Someone Who

Review the vocabulary with your teacher. • Fill in the name of someone who . . .

1. _____ has a sweatsuit.
2. _____ is wearing sneakers.
3. _____ bought a new soccer ball.
4. _____ works at a sporting goods store.
5. _____ likes to wear a baseball cap.
6. _____ would like to buy golf clubs.

TOY STORE

1. bicycle	7. doll	13. paint set	19. toy kitchen
2. board game	8. duck	14. penguin	20. tricycle
3. car	9. electric train	15. rubber ball	21. truck
4. chess set	10. fire engine	16. snake	
5. computer game	11. mobile	17. stuffed animal	
6. darts	12. model airplane	18. teddy bear	

See Conversation Springboards on pages 104 and 105.

Partner Interview

Partner's Name _____

Practice these questions with your teacher. • Then ask your partner.
1. When you were a child, did you have a favorite toy? What was it?
2. What children's toys were popular in your country when you were a child? What is popular now?
3. What do children like to play with where you live now?
4. Do you buy toys? Where do you buy them?

Group Decision

Work in groups of four. • Decide what toy to buy for each of these children. • Report your decisions to the class.
1. a baby girl
2. a two-year-old boy
3. an eight-year-old boy
4. a five-year-old girl
5. a ten-year-old girl

Group Survey

Ask everyone in your group these questions. • Check YES or NO. • Count the answers. • Report your group's results to the class. • Write the class' results on the board.

When you were a child . . .	YES	NO
1. did you ever play with dolls?	_____	_____
2. did you ever ride a tricycle?	_____	_____
3. did you like to color?	_____	_____
4. did you like to play ball?	_____	_____
5. did you like to read?	_____	_____

SHOE STORE

1. baby shoes	10. length	19. shoe polish	28. winter boots
2. canvas	11. loafers	20. shoe size	29. work boots
3. cheap	12. man-made materials	21. shoe tree	
4. expensive	13. moccasins	22. sole	
5. fit	14. narrow (N)	23. suede	
6. flats	15. plastic	24. walking shoes	
7. heel	16. rubber boots	25. Western boots	
8. high heels	17. shoe box	26. wide (W)	
9. leather	18. shoe horn	27. width	

Group Role Play

Work in groups of five. • Write a role play for the scene. • Include roles for everyone. • Present your role play to the class.

See Conversation Springboards on page 105.

Find Someone Who

Review the vocabulary with your teacher. • *Fill in the name of someone who . . .*

1. _____ has more than ten pairs of shoes.
2. _____ wants Western boots.
3. _____ buys expensive shoes.
4. _____ wears the same size shoes as you do.
5. _____ has more than one pair of work shoes.

Group Discussion

Work in groups of five. • *Discuss these questions.* • *Report your answers to the class.*

1. How many pairs of shoes do you have?
2. Where do you buy your shoes?
3. What shoes do you wear to work?
4. What shoes do you wear to school?
5. What shoes do you wear to go dancing?
6. What kind of shoes do you wear in cold weather?
7. Which shoes are your favorite shoes?
8. What is your shoe size?

Cross-Cultural Exchange

What kinds of shoes are popular in your country? • *Are shoe sizes in your country different from shoe sizes in the United States?* • *Are shoes made in your country?* • *What kinds?*

MEN'S CLOTHING STORE

1. bathrobe
2. cap
3. casual wear
4. dress shirt
5. extra large (XL)
6. large (L)
7. long sleeves
8. medium (M)
9. short sleeves
10. small (S)
11. sweat pants
12. turtleneck
13. undershirt
14. wallet
_____
_____

Partner Interview   Partner's Name _____

Practice these questions with your teacher. • *Then ask your partner.*

1. Where is the men's store in your neighborhood?
2. What can you buy in the store?
3. When do you shop for men's clothes?
4. Who do you buy men's clothing for?

Group Decision

Work in groups of five or six. • *Decide what clothing the men in the picture will buy for the following activities.* • *Report your decisions to the class.*

1. jogging
2. a job interview
3. a wedding
4. fixing a car
5. going to a movie
6. going to class

See Conversation Springboards on page 105.

WOMEN'S CLOTHING STORE

1. bra/brassiere
2. clothing rack
3. hat rack
4. headband
5. hosiery
6. nightgown
7. price tag
8. robe
9. shopping bag
10. slacks (pants)
11. slip
12. tights
13. try on
_____
_____
_____

Partner Vocabulary Challenge   Partner's Name _____

Make a list of the other vocabulary words in this picture. • *How many words do you remember?*
• *Compare your list with another pair of students.* • *Add to your list.*

Group Decision

Work in groups of five or six. • *With your group, decide what one of these women will buy today.* •
Report your decisions to the class.

1. What is her name?
2. Why is she shopping today?
3. What will she try on?
4. What new clothes will she buy?
5. How much money will she spend?
6. How will she pay for the clothes?

Community Activity

Bring in newspaper ads for women's clothing. • *Choose one item to buy.* • *How much does it cost?* • *Make a list on the board of the items everyone in the class wants to buy.* • *List the prices.* • *Who wanted the most expensive item? the least expensive?* • *What was the most popular item?*

See Conversation Springboards on page 105.

REVIEW

Partner Game: *"What do you remember?"*   Partner's Name _____

Look at the shopping mall on pages 82 and 83 with your partner. • Remember as much as you can. • Close your book. • Describe the scene with your partner. • List everything. • Compare your notes with another pair. • Add to your list.

Partner Activity   Partner's Name _____

You won a shopping spree for $500 at the mall! • Decide together how to spend the money. • Make a list, including the shops you will visit, what you will buy, and how much each item will cost. • Report your decision to another pair.

Community Activity

In groups of four, decide on recommendations for the best places to shop in your community. • Tell the class about your recommendations. • Explain your choices.

	Name of Store	Reason for Shopping
1. mall		
2. sporting goods store		
3. toy store		
4. shoe store		
5. men's clothing store		
6. women's clothing store		

Class Activity

List ten questions about shopping. • Write them on the board.

Partner Activity   Partner's Name _____

Ask your partner the questions from the Class Activity. • Present your interview to the class.

APPENDIX

Conversation Springboards	**94**
Grammar for Conversation	**106**
Maps	
Africa	118
Asia and Australia	119
Europe	120
North, Central, and South America	121
United States of America (U.S.A.) and Canada	122
Nations/Nationalities	**123**
Names/Nicknames	**124**
Gossip Secrets	**125**
Speech/Audience Evaluation Forms	**125**
Alphabetical Word List to Picture Dictionary	**126**

CONVERSATION SPRINGBOARDS

UNIT 1: WELCOME TO CLASS
WELCOME TO CLASS! (pp. 2-3)
Conversation 1: *What's happening?*

A: Here's my picture!
B: Oh, I like it. Tell me about it.
A: Well, I'm a woman, of course! I have long, straight hair and green eyes.
B: But your hair is short and curly now.
A: Well, you know, people change... Tell me about your picture!
B: All right. Well, of course, I'm a man. I have a moustache and glasses—and brown, wavy hair.
A: But you don't have a moustache now!
B: Well, like you said, people change, you know.

Conversation 2: *What's next?*

A: Hi. I'm Keiko. What's your name?
B: Hi, Keiko. My name's Maria. Nice to meet you.
A: You, too. I like your earrings, Maria.
B: Thanks. They're very old. Keiko, do you know the man with the glasses?
A: Uh-huh.
B: What's his name?
A: That's Paco. He's nice.
B: Would you introduce me?
A: Sure. He's single, you know.
B: Really? Hmm...

COUNTRIES (pp. 4-5)
Conversation 1: *What's the process?*

A: Hi. Are you my partner?
B: Yes, I am. What's your name?
A: My name's Paco. What's yours?
B: Don. Don Park. What's your last name, Paco?
A: Montero.
B: How do you spell Montero?
A: M-O-N-T-E-R-O. Where are you from, Don?
B: Seoul, Korea. Where are you from?
A: Colombia. Where's Korea, Don?
B: It's in northern Asia. Where's Colombia?
A: It's in South America. What language do Koreans speak?
B: We speak Korean. What language do Colombians speak, Paco?
A: We speak Spanish.
B: OK. Great! We're finished!

Conversation 2: *What's your opinion?*

A: Where do you want to visit?
B: I want to go to Europe.
A: Where in Europe?
B: Oh, Spain, France, Germany, Italy... Actually, I want to see all the countries in Europe.
A: What cities do you want to visit?
B: I want to see Paris. It's so beautiful.
A: You're right, it is. I'm from Paris.
B: Are you really?!

NUMBERS (p. 6)
Conversation: *What's the process?*

A: Let's do a class survey!
B: That sounds like fun! How many students are there?
A: Let's count. Who's absent?
B: No one. We're all here. One, two, three, four, five, six, seven, eight, nine, ten, eleven, twelve—there are twelve of us.
A: Six women and four men, plus us; that's eight women and four men. How many wear glasses?
B: One, two, three, four. Four are wearing glasses.
A: How many men are bald?
B: Zero. Nobody is bald. Everyone has hair.

JOURNAL (p. 7)
Conversation: *What's the process?*

A: Are you ready for our Partner Interview?
B: Yes. You start.
A: OK. What's your name, please?
B: It's Ani Lee. And yours?
A: Sam Young. Nice to meet you, Ani.
B: You, too. What's today's date?
A: April 7. How many students are in our class?
B: Hmm, I think fifteen...
A: Fifty?!
B: No, no! Fifteen.
A: Oh, fifteen. Next question: Are you married?
B: No, I'm single. And you?
A: I'm divorced. OK, next question: Where are you from?
B: I'm from Taipei, Taiwan. What about you?
A: I'm from Pusan, Korea. So, I speak Korean and you speak Chinese, right?
B: That's right. Taiwanese and Mandarin. There, we're done!

CLOTHING AND COLORS (p. 8)
Conversation: *What's the process?*

A: Are you ready for the Partner Game activity, Paul?
B: Sure, Joe. What do we do?
A: You look at my clothes—I look at your clothes—then we sit back to back and list what we remember.
B: OK, that's easy. I'm ready.
A: What do you remember?
B: Let's see. You're wearing a white T-shirt and red shorts.
A: What else?
B: What else? Umm... I don't remember the color of your shoes.
A: They're white.
B: Oh, of course—running shoes. OK, now it's your turn.

PAIRS OF CLOTHING (p. 9)
Conversation: *What's next?*

A: Welcome to our fashion show. Here is Maria, our first model.
B: Maria is Brazilian, and today she's wearing a beautiful, light green sweater and gold pants.

A: Maria also has on a brown belt and a lovely yellow scarf with polka dots. She has a gold barrette in her hair, and she's wearing green sandals.
Audience: Yea, Maria! Way to go, Maria!
B: Thank you, Maria! Now here's model number two, Adisorn, from Thailand. Adisorn is wearing blue jeans, a purple sweat shirt, and a pair of sneakers with yellow socks.
Audience: All right, Adisorn! Yea!
A: OK. Thanks, Adisorn. Now here's our next model, Olga, from Russia. She's wearing a light pink blouse and red skirt. Her red sunglasses look great with her pretty blouse and skirt.
Audience: Yea! Beautiful! Yea, Olga!
B: All our models have interesting clothes today. Now, who's next?

FAMILY (pp. 10-11)

Conversation 1: What's happening?

A: I'm glad you have your family photos today, George. I have mine, too.
B: Great! Tell me about your photos first, Cindy.
A: Well, this one is my whole family: my parents and grandparents, my sister and her family, and me, too.
B: Who's who?
A: Here's my grandmother, and this is my grandfather. And this is my mother, and here's my father.
B: Is this your sister? She's so young!
A: Yes, she's my younger sister. These are her two kids, my niece and nephew.
B: What a great photo! You have a very nice family, Cindy.

Conversation 2: What's the process?

A: Let's do the Partner Interview, Chris.
B: All right. You start, Naomi.
A: OK. Is your family big or small?
B: It's small. There are four people in my family.
A: How many brothers and sisters do you have?
B: I have one older brother. No sisters.
A: Do you have any children?
B: No. I'm not married yet. But, I have two dogs and three cats.
A: No kidding! Do you really have five pets?
B: Yes, I do. I love animals!

UNIT 2: EVERYDAY LIFE

THE CLASSROOM (pp. 14-15)

Conversation 1: What's next?

A: Hi, Maria. Is it OK if I sit next to you?
B: Sure, Paco, have a seat. I'm reviewing today's lesson from English class. Do you want to review with me?
A: Uh. . . sure. . . good idea.
B: OK. Let's name all the things in the classroom.
A: Let's see. . . There's a big window, a chalkboard, chalk, the teacher's desk, a chair, and a door.
B: Don't forget the clock and the globe, and, of course, desks for all of us!
A: Right! What about things we use?
B: Let's see. . . notebooks, erasers, pens, pencils, paper, and books.
A: Maria, it's fun to study with you.
B: I like it, too, Paco. . .

Conversation 2: What's the process?

A: Time for the Group Game, everyone. Yuki, you be the leader.
B: OK. Let me think of something. . . OK, I'm ready.
C: Is it on the board?
B: No, it's not on the board.
D: Is it on the teacher's desk?
B: No, it's not on the teacher's desk.
C: Is it big?
B: Well, not very big. . . It's pretty big.
A: Let's see, it's not on the board, and it's not on the teacher's desk. . . Is it on the wall?
B: Yes, it's on the wall.
A: Is it the clock?
B: Yes, it is! Good guess! You're the new leader now.

TAKING A BREAK (pp. 16-17)

Conversation 1: What's happening?

A: Look at Jerry—he's sleeping! He's always tired.
B: Well, he has three jobs. Mark's tired, too. See? He's yawning.
A: Hey, what's wrong with Karen? She's crying!
B: Yeah, she looks pretty upset. Listen to Joe—he's arguing with Vanessa and Tim again. They're always arguing!
A: Unbelievable! But, not Steve. Look—he's laughing. He's always laughing about something.
B: Yeah. Hey, guess who Andrew is drawing on the board!
A: That's funny! Is it George?
B: It sure looks like George. Where is George? I don't see him.
Teacher: OK, class. Break's over.

Conversation 2: What's next?

A: I'm glad we're finally taking a break. I'm thirsty!
B: Yeah. It's really hot in the classroom!
A: I need a nice cold glass of water.
B: Me, too!
A: I'm worried tonight. We have a test after the break, you know.
B: I know. I always get nervous about tests.
A: You, too, huh? Oh, my, look at Al! He looks sick!
B: Al, are you OK?
C: Oh. . . I don't know. . .

TIME (pp. 18-19)

Conversation 1: *What's happening?*

A: What time do you go to bed, Gino?
B: Oh, around twelve.
A: Midnight! Are you kidding? That's too late!
B: Well, what time do you go to bed, Sue?
A: About 10:30. I love waking up early and watching the sunrise.
B: Not me! I like studying late at night, going to bed late, and sleeping late.
A: Maybe that's why you're always late to class.
B: And you're always early.
A: Yes, I'm really a morning person.
B: And I'm definitely a night person!

Conversation 2: *What's the process?*

A: OK, guys. Let's do the Group Survey. The class is almost over.
B, C, D: OK. Yeah, sure. All right, let's do it. . .
A: First question: Do you get up early in the morning?
B: Yes, I do.
C: No, I don't.
D: I do.
A: And I do, too. OK, that's three yesses and one no. Question two: Do you get up before 7:00 a.m.?
C: No! Are you kidding?!
B: Yes, I do.
D: I do, too.
A: Me, too. That's three yesses and one no again. Question 3: Do you go to bed late at night? (*Bell rings*).
B: Time to go!
A: Come on, guys. Let's finish this question.
C: Yeah, what's the hurry?
D: We have a class—we want to be on time!

EVERYDAY LIFE (pp. 20-21)

Conversation 1: *What's the process?*

A: Our daily lives are so different, Lucy. You have five kids, and you're here on time for class every day!
B: Yep, that's my life, Charlie.
A: How do you do it? I'm single and I'm always late!
B: Well, I get up early. The children go to school early. Then I do the housework. At 8:00 I go to school. No problem.
A: No problem for you!
B: What about you, Charlie?
A: Me? I sleep late because I study late at night. When do you do your homework, Lucy?
B: I do mine late at night, too. I guess our lives are the same in one way.

Conversation 2: *What's the process?*

Teacher: OK, class, this activity is called Find Someone Who. Let's try one together. Tom, do you wash the dishes every evening?
A: No way! My wife does the dishes!
Teacher: How about you, Rita? Do you wash the dishes every evening?
B: No, I don't. I make dinner, and my kids wash the dishes.
Teacher: Jerry, do you wash the dishes every evening?
C: Yes, I do. My wife works at night, and I make dinner and wash the dishes.
Teacher: Good. Now fill in Jerry's name on the line. J-E-R-R-Y. Any questions?
Students: No. I'm fine. No problem.
Teacher: OK. Stand up, walk around, and ask questions. Sit down when you're finished. You have ten minutes.

MORNING ROUTINE (pp. 22-23)

Conversation 1: *What's happening?*

A: The guy in the book is so funny! Do you have the same morning routine as he does, Anna?
B: No, my morning routine is very different.
A: How?
B: Well, first of all, I always get up really early, at five o'clock.
A: That *is* early!
B: And, of course, I don't shave. I usually take a bath, not a shower.
A: Do you always make your bed?
B: Sometimes. Do you?
A: No, I never make my bed!

Conversation 2: *What's happening?*

A: Do you watch the morning news on TV, Sally?
B: Sometimes. I like to watch the news and drink my coffee. What about you, Mohammed?
A: I never watch the morning news. I'm always in a hurry.
B: Why?
A: Because I don't like to get out of bed in the morning.
B: I like to stay in bed sometimes, too. I like to watch TV in bed.
A: You, too? I always watch TV in bed. But I never watch the news.
B: No? Well, I watch the news and drink my coffee in bed. *Then* I get up.

UNIT 3: THE CALENDAR

DAYS OF THE WEEK (pp. 26-27)

Conversation 1: *What's the process?*

A: You're my partner, Henry. Where's your calendar?
B: Here it is, but I don't understand what to do. Can you help me?
A: Yeah, sure. Start with yesterday, Sunday. What did you do?
B: I visited my family in the afternoon, and I studied in the evening.
A: OK. Write "visit family" in the Sunday afternoon box. All right. Now write "study" in the Sunday evening box.
B: I see. Thanks. So, today, Monday, I write "class" in the Monday morning box, "lunch with friends" in the afternoon box, and "work" in the evening box. Right?
A: Exactly! Not so hard, is it?
B: No, I guess not. Thanks, Jim!

Conversation 2: *What happened?*

A: What did you do last weekend, Al?
B: Oh, nothing special. I worked Saturday. Then, yesterday, I studied most of the day, and watched the basketball game on TV last night. What about you, Becky?
A: Your weekend sounds wonderful to me, Al! Mine was terrible.
B: Really? What happened?
A: Well, Friday evening I had a big fight with my boyfriend. Saturday I had a headache all day, and I felt terrible.
B: Gee, I'm sorry. What about Sunday?
A: Well, I wanted to study Sunday, but I lost my English book. So, I didn't do my homework, and now I don't have a book!
B: Really? I found an extra English book in my backpack this weekend. See? There's no name in it. Maybe it's yours.
A: Oh, it *is* my book! That's my writing in the vocabulary boxes! Thank you, Al. You made my day!

MONTHS AND DATES (pp. 28-29)
Conversation 1: *What's the process?*

A: OK, group, what are some important dates?
B: Hmm... Let's see. How about this one: January 1st—the first day of the year.
A: That's a good one. What are some others?
C: How about February 14th? It's Valentine's Day.
A: Great! Now we have two dates. Let's get some more.
D: I know one. November 17th is a very important day!
B: November 17th? That's today. Why is today so important?
D: It's my first anniversary!
A, B, C: Happy anniversary!

Conversation 2: *What's your opinion?*

A: What's your favorite month, Bill?
B: I don't know. I don't think I have a favorite month, Pete. Do you?
A: Yeah, June is my favorite month. My birthday's June third.
B: Really?! My birthday's on the third, too, but July third.
A: There's another reason I like June best. I always take my vacation then—the second week in June. By the way, do you know what date this course ends?
B: Yes, June ninth.
A: Great! I'll start my vacation on June tenth.
B: I usually take my vacation in July. You know, I guess I do have a favorite month—July!

BIRTHDAYS (pp. 30-31)
Conversation 1: *What's happening?*

A: Let's hurry and finish up. She's coming home soon.
B: Quick, Jan! Light the candles!
C: No, not yet. It's too soon.
D: Oh! There are no cups on the table! And where are the napkins?
C: Don't worry, they're right here.
D: OK.
A: Oh, no! She's here! She's at the door!
B: But the candles, the candles! (*Door opens.*)
A, B, C, D: Surprise!
(*singing*)
Happy birthday to you,
Happy birthday to you,
Happy birthday, dear Teacher,
Happy birthday to you.

Conversation 2: *What's the process?*

A: When's your birthday, Raymond?
B: August 20th. When's yours?
A: February 28th. What's a good message for a birthday card?
B: I don't know. "Happy birthday," I guess.
A: But it already says "happy birthday." I want to write something more, something special.
B: How about... umm... I got it! How about this: "You're a very special friend. Have a great birthday!"
A: I like it! How do you spell "special"?
B: S-p-e... uh... How about "You're a very good friend," instead?
A: Fine. I know how to spell that.

HOLIDAYS (pp. 32-33)
Conversation 1: *What's the process?*

A: OK, I'm finished writing. These Conversation Squares are easy.
B: I'm ready, too. Let's ask the questions now.
C: Not yet! I'm not finished!
A: That's OK, Sue. Take your time. Christina and I can begin. What's your favorite holiday, Christina?
B: Halloween. I love Halloween parties! Every year I wear a different costume. Last year I was an ugly witch.
A: Good. That's a "holiday activity." What about "holiday food"?
B: Hmm... The only special food I know for Halloween is candy. Is that OK?
A: Sure.
C: OK, I'm ready now. What did you say, Christina?

Conversation 2: *What's the process?*

A: Can you help me with the speech I'm giving today?
B: Sure, I'd be glad to. Let's see, the topic is "Holidays in My Country." What holiday do you want to talk about?
A: Hmm... How about Independence Day?
B: Sounds good. What happens on that day?
A: Well, there's no work or school. Everyone has a day off.
B: Right, but what are the customs?
A: There's always a parade with marching bands, and families get together.
B: What about fireworks?
A: I almost forgot! That's my favorite thing—I always watch the fireworks!

SEASONS (pp. 34-35)
Conversation 1: *What's happening?*
A: What are the seasons like in your hometown, Maria?
B: Oh, they are very different from here. Remember, I come from Brazil!
A: So, what are the seasons like in Brazil?
B: Well, summer is in December, January, and February. So, Christmas is very hot and sunny.
A: That *is* very different! Summer in my country is June, July, and August. What's winter like in Brazil?
B: It depends on where in Brazil. Some places are cold and rainy, and some are just cool.
A: Does it snow?
B: Not really. If we want snow, we go to Chile.

Conversation 2: *What's the process?*
A: OK, it's time to close the book now. What do you remember from the picture, Elizabeth?
B: Not much, Linda.
A: Why? We looked at the picture.
B: Oh, I remember the picture. But I forget the words. Vocabulary is very difficult for me.
A: Ah, I understand. I'll start, then. You write the words. You know, writing is good practice for vocabulary.
B: OK, good idea. So, what do you remember, Linda?
A: I remember a frozen man in a big block of ice.
B: And I remember a snowman!
A: You do remember vocabulary! That's great, Liz!

WEATHER (pp. 36-37)
Conversation 1: *What's the process?*
A: OK, Partner Interview again. Of course, I know your name already, Kati. Let me write it in. . .
B: I'll start, OK? What do you like to do on a rainy day, Jun?
A: I like to stay in bed and read all day. I feel lazy on a rainy day! What do you like to do on a rainy day, Kati?
B: Believe it or not, I like to go out for a walk in the rain. I take my dog with me. She likes it, too!
A: Really?! Don't you get wet?
B: A little. But I wear my raincoat, and I have an umbrella. My dog wears a raincoat, too! It's fun, really. Why don't you come with us next time?
A: No, thanks. I think I'll stay in bed. (*Bell rings*.)
B: Oh, no—the bell! We never get to finish!

Conversation 2: *What happened?*
A: How was your weekend, Gene?
B: Crazy! I had a real adventure! My family and I were on a picnic, and there was a hailstorm!
A: Oh, no! What did you do?
B: We hid under the picnic table. The hail was as big as golf balls!
A: You're kidding!
B: No, really. We ate lunch under the table.
A: I had an adventure in the desert one time. I was riding a horse, and there was a dust storm.
B: Oh, no! What did you do?
A: Well, my horse stopped, of course. I just closed my eyes and hid my face and waited for the storm to pass. It was awful! I couldn't breathe!
B: It sounds worse than a hailstorm!

WEATHER REPORT (p. 38)
Conversation: *What's next?*
Meteorologist: . . . And the weather for the Northwest today was cloudy and cool.
A: Boy, I'm glad we don't live in the Northwest. It's always cloudy and cool there!
B: And rainy!
A: This is my kind of weather here—hot and sunny all summer!
Meteorologist: Tomorrow, the Northeast is getting severe thunderstorms.
A: Oh, no! I want to go to the beach tomorrow!
B: Me, too. Maybe the meteorologist is wrong.
A: Well, if he's right, let's go to the movies!

SEASONAL CLOTHING (p. 39)
Conversation: *What's happening?*
A: This is my first winter here in Boston. It's so cold, and I don't know what to wear!
B: I see that, Joshua! You're shivering! You definitely need a heavy winter jacket.
A: I think you're right, Jenny. This jacket was fine in my country, but this weather is too cold and windy for it!
B: Buy some gloves and boots and a wool hat, too. Some people like earmuffs instead of hats.
A: What about long underwear?
B: If it's very cold and you're outdoors, long underwear is a good idea.
A: Thanks for the advice, Jenny. But when does it get warm here?
B: *Really* warm? Not for five more months! Put away your shorts and bathing suits until June!

UNIT 4: FOOD
FRUIT (pp. 42-43)
Conversation 1: *What's next?*
A: What's your favorite fruit, Jeff?
B: Oh, I love all kinds of fruit, Gail.
A: Me, too. But what do you like best?
B: Well, I think maybe oranges.
A: Mmm. I like oranges, too. What other fruits do you like?
B: Grapefruit. I love grapefruit. And cherries—but I don't like the pits.
A: How about grapes and watermelon?
B: Yes, but not the seeds. I like seedless grapes and seedless watermelon better. Boy, this conversation is making me hungry for some fruit!
A: Me, too!

Conversation 2: *What's the process?*
A: Hey, let's make a fruit salad!
B, C, D: Great idea! Sounds good! Yeah!
B: OK. We can each bring something for the salad.

C: I'll bring a bowl and a large spoon.
D: I'll bring a knife—I have a sharp knife.
B: I'll bring plates and forks.
A: What about the fruit? My favorites are oranges and grapefruit.
D: Mmm-hmm! And I love melons—watermelon and cantaloupe!
C: Don't forget grapes and bananas and apples.
B: Bring everything tomorrow, and we'll make the fruit salad for lunch.
A, C, D: Yum! Sounds great! All right!

VEGETABLES (pp. 44-45)

Conversation 1: *What's happening?*

A: Hi. Can I help you?
B: Yes. What vegetables are good today?
A: Let's see. . . everything is good, but the corn and the cabbage are especially fresh.
B: That corn does look good! I'll take a half dozen ears, please.
A: Yes, the corn is a good buy. It's in season. Anything else?
B: The tomatoes look great. I'll take four. And a head of lettuce.
A: How about some beans? They just came in this morning.
B: OK. A pound of beans. That's all for today. By the way, what's your dog's name?
A: Veggie. He loves all kinds of vegetables. Here, Veggie, want a carrot?
Dog: Woof! Woof!

Conversation 2: *What's the process?*

A: We'd like to show you our salad. This is how we made it. We each brought in a different vegetable and prepared it together.
B: I brought in a head of lettuce.
C: Carol and I washed the lettuce. Then I shredded it and put it in the bowl.
D: I brought in a bunch of carrots. I peeled them and cut them up.
C: I cooked the beets and sliced them at home.
A: I don't like vegetables, but I brought in some mushrooms, anyway.
D: We mixed all the vegetables together, and then we added salad dressing.
B: And here it is! We hope you enjoy it!

MEAT, SEAFOOD, AND POULTRY (pp. 46-47)

Conversation 1: *What's next?*

A: I'm glad you're coming for dinner tonight, Paco. Do you eat poultry?
B: Do you mean chicken?
A: Yes, chicken or turkey. Which do you prefer? Or would you prefer red meat?
B: Well, Maria, I don't really eat red meat.
A: I don't eat much red meat, either. How about some seafood? Fish? Shrimp?
B: Well. . . I don't really care too much for fish, either, Maria.
A: That's OK. How about pork chops, then?

B: Actually, Maria, I'm a vegetarian. I don't usually eat any meat at all. But I know I'll like anything you cook!

Conversation 2: *What's the process?*

A: Karen, do you understand this Find Someone Who?
B: I think so.
A: We need to find classmates who like food a certain way, right?
B: Yes. Let's start with you, Don. Do you like baked fish with salt and pepper?
A: Well, I like salt and pepper, but I don't like baked fish!
B: OK. Now I'll ask Steve. Oh, Steve, do you like baked fish with salt and pepper?
C: Yes, I love it! Now, let me ask you and Don Question Two. Do you like barbecued spare ribs?
B: What's that?
C: I'm not sure! Do you know what they are, Don?
A: Yeah, I think they're. . . umm. . . Let's ask the teacher.

DESSERTS (pp. 48-49)

Conversation 1: *What's the process?*

A: How do we do this activity?
B: First, we fill in the menu with desserts we all like.
C: I'll start with brownies. And what about the prices?
D: Let's fill in all the desserts first, and then do the prices.
B: OK. How about apple pie with ice cream?
A: That's called apple pie a la mode. Let's add sherbet.
C: And frozen yogurt. That's popular these days.
D: How many desserts do we have now?
A: Four. We need one more. How about some chocolate chip cookies?
B: Great! The menu's ready. Oh, wait a minute! We didn't do the prices! (*Bell rings*.)
Teacher: That's it for today. We'll continue this activity tomorrow—same groups.

Conversation 2: *What's your opinion?*

A: This looks like a great class! Look at all those desserts!
B: Here's the dessert I brought in. It's called "anpan." It's a pastry filled with red bean paste. It's from Japan.
C: That looks delicious. Mine is from Puerto Rico. It's "flan."
D: Well, look at mine! It looks the same. It's called "crème brûlée" and is very popular in France.
C: It does look the same as mine! What's in it?
D: It's made with milk and eggs. It's a custard.
C: It *is* the same! I can't wait to taste it!
Teacher: I know you are all waiting for this: break time!
Students: Oh, great! Delicious! Mmm! Wonderful!

BREAKFAST (pp. 50-51)

Conversation 1: *What's your opinion?*

A: What do you eat for breakfast, Paul?
B: Not much, really. Usually I have a glass of orange juice and vitamins. I always take vitamins in the morning.
A: Do you eat anything else for breakfast?
B: Sometimes I have a piece of toast.
C: I always have a big breakfast: eggs, bacon, home fries, coffee, and juice. I love American breakfasts.
A: I do, too, Sam, but they make me fat.
C: What do you eat for breakfast, Kathy?
A: I have juice, nonfat yogurt, and toast. It's better for my health.

Conversation 2: *What's the process?*

A: Conversation Squares again! OK, first we write our own answers.
B: I wrote my answers already.
C: Me, too.
A: All right. Let's ask the questions, then. What did you have for breakfast today, Van Yen?
B: I had noodle soup.
A: Noodle soup! Really?
B: Oh, yes. It's very good. I always have noodle soup for breakfast. What did you have, Jack?
A: Hot cereal and cocoa. It's my favorite in the winter. I have it every day. What about you, Mimi?
C: Just a cup of coffee. I never eat anything for breakfast.
A: So we each have the same breakfast every day.
C: Yes, but we don't all *have* the same breakfast!

LUNCH (pp. 52-53)

Conversation 1: *What's happening?*

A: I'm so hungry! I skipped lunch today, and now I'm really hungry!
B: I never skip lunch, Ken.
A: Well, I'm sorry I did. What did you have for lunch, Jim?
B: Spaghetti and meatballs.
A: That sounds wonderful! Where did you go for lunch?
B: Oh, I just ate at work. We have a microwave oven there. I always bring in leftovers and warm them up.
A: That's a good idea. Do you like to cook?
B: No, but my mother is a great cook. She always makes lots of food, and I have leftovers for lunch.
A: Lucky you! Does your mother want another son?

Conversation 2: *What's happening?*

A: What's for lunch, Paco?
B: Sandwiches.
A: Oh, good. I love sandwiches.
B: What would you like on yours, Maria?
A: What do you have?
B: Everything—cold cuts, tuna fish, cheese, peanut butter—you name it! We have three kinds of bread, too.
A: Great! Do you have sliced turkey?
B: Sure do. What kind of bread? White? Wheat? Rye?
A: Rye, please. And could I have some lettuce, tomato, and mayonnaise with that?
B: You bet.
A: What a beautiful sandwich! Thanks, Paco.

FAST FOOD (pp. 54-55)

Conversation 1: *What's the process?*

A: Do you think fast food is bad for you, Heather?
B: Yes, of course. I like fast food, but I know it's bad for me.
A: OK, that's it! We're finished with the Group Survey questions.
C: Now we count the answers, right?
A: Right. I have four "yesses" and three "nos" for Number 1.
B: No, that's not right! I have three "yesses" and four "nos."
C: And I have four "yesses" and four "nos"!
D: That can't be right. There are only seven people in our group. What do we do now?
C: Count again. Or ask the questions again, raise our hands, and count together.
A, B, D: Oh, boy! Not again!

Conversation 2: *What's the process?*

A: Role plays are difficult to write, aren't they?
B: Do you think so? I think they're easy.
A: Easy? Really? I'm glad you're my partner, Victor.
B: OK. Let's see now. . . The cashier says "May I help you?"
A: Why doesn't he say "Can I help you?"
B: Because it says "May I help you" in the book.
A: But is "Can I help you?" OK? I hear people say "Can I help you?" in stores all the time.
B: Yes, that's true. You can say that. But I think "May I help you?" is a little more polite.
A: Really? But, can we change it, anyway?
B: I think I understand why role plays are difficult for you to write, Lisa.

JUNK FOOD (p. 56)

Conversation: *What's next?*

A: Coffee break! Junk food time! I'm going to the vending machines. Want something, Bob?
B: No thanks, Mary.
A: Don't you ever eat junk food?
B: Not from these vending machines!
A: Why not?
B: Last week I lost money in the machine three times! Nothing came out—no soda, no coffee, no money back.
A: That's too bad! What did you do?
B: I kicked the machine a few times, but nothing happened.
A: Well, I hope it works today. I'm really hungry for a chocolate bar! Wish me luck!

DINNER (p. 57)

Conversation: *What's next?*

A: I'm glad we came to this restaurant, David. It's beautiful!
B: It *is* nice, isn't it? Margaret, there's something I want to talk to you about.
A: Really? What is it, David?
B: Well, we've known each other for three years now.
A: Uh-huh.

B: And we like each other. . . a lot.
A: Yes, we do.
B: Well, I. . .
C: David! Margaret! What a surprise! Hey, Annie, it's David and Margaret! Oh, this is great! Let's have dinner together!
D: Wait, Jack—maybe David and Margaret want to eat alone.
B: No, no. . . that's. . . that's fine, Annie. It's. . . it's good to see you, *really*.

THE SUPERMARKET (pp. 58-59)

Conversation 1: *What's happening?*

A: You push the cart, OK? Thanks, honey.
B: Sure. What's on the shopping list?
A: Let's see. . . bread, pickles, eggs, ketchup.
B: How much bread do we need?
A: Oh, one loaf is fine, dear. And just a small jar of pickles.
B: OK. Which aisle are the pickles in?
A: Aisle Two. And get a dozen eggs, honey. They're at the end of the aisle.
B: A large bottle of ketchup, right?
A: Yes, I love ketchup! Thanks for shopping with me today, dear. It's fun to shop together, isn't it? . . . Dear? I said, isn't it fun to shop together?
B: Oh, yes, right. Lots of fun. . .

Conversation 2: *What's the process?*

A: What's this Vocabulary Challenge activity?
B: We have to make a list of things from the supermarket.
C: And work fast.
A: That sounds easy. But I don't want to write the words. I can't spell.
C: OK, I'll write. What are some things?
Students: Milk, meat, fish, oranges, apples, margarine, napkins, salt, pepper, rice, potatoes. . . Don't forget lettuce, carrots, beans, celery, chicken, turkey, mayonnaise, cookies. . .
C: Wait a minute, wait a minute! I can't write that fast!! Now start again. What did you say—milk? (*Buzzer sounds*).
Teacher: OK, class. Time's up. How many words do you have?

UNIT 5: HOMES

CITY OR COUNTRY (pp. 62-63)

Conversation 1: *What's next?*

A: First question on the Group Discussion. Do you like where you live now?
B: Yes, I do.
C: I don't. I liked my hometown better.
D: I do. I love living here.
A: And my answer is yes, too. OK. Second question: In our opinion, where is the best place in the world to live?
D: Definitely Alaska. You can ski all the time!
B: I think right here. I love the city—it's so exciting.
C: No, I hate the city. It's so noisy! The best place is in the country. It's calm and peaceful.
A: Or by the ocean. I love the water. I'd like to live on the coast.
B: Uh-oh. The last question asks us to decide as a group which place we like best. How will we ever agree on that?!

Conversation 2: *What's the process?*

A: Time for the "Gossip!" game. This will be fun! OK, we need to choose a leader. How about if Pat is the leader?
Students: Sure! OK. Great!
B: Now, everyone, close your books. Tom, you read the secret on page 125. . .
C: OK. I read it. Now what?
B: Now tell the secret to the person sitting next to you; tell Maria the secret.
C: I came to the U.S. when I was 15 with my mother and father and two brothers. We lived on a busy street in the city. Our street was noisy. It was exciting to be in a big city because I was born on a farm in the country. I still love the city.
B: Now, Maria, tell the person next to you. Remember to whisper!
D: I was born in the countryside. It was beautiful and quiet. I moved to the U.S. when I was 15. We lived in the city. It was noisy. I still love the city.
B: OK, great. Now, Kan, tell the next person.
E: I love the city even though it's noisy and dirty. I was born in a beautiful town in the country. Umm. Boy, this is hard. I can't remember all the details!

HOMES (pp. 64-65)

Conversation 1: *What's your opinion?*

A: What do you think of the homes around here?
B: Well, they sure are different from the homes in the place where I was born.
A: Why? What do you mean?
B: Well, in my hometown, all the homes were private homes. And most of them were made of stucco.
A: Did you have a yard and a porch?
B: Yes. Actually, my parents still live there. There's a balcony, too.
A: Wow. It sounds beautiful. Here there are so many apartments and condos! And we live in dormitories! Hardly a private house at all.
B: Yes, and out on the highway, there are so many mobile home parks.
A: Well, that's a lot different from the neighborhood where I grew up.

Conversation 2: *What's happening?*

A: What do you think of the new high-rise in our neighborhood?
B: I really like it! I saw a model apartment. The floors are all wood, and there are fireplaces in every apartment!
A: And some of the apartments have balconies. I think there's a terrace garden on the roof, too.
B: There are trees and flowers—on the roof!
A: Do you think there's a basement? A lot of new buildings don't have basements!
B: Are you kidding? In this building they have everything! It's like having your own house!
A: I guess so, but I'd rather have my own little house to call home.
B: Not me. I wish I had enough money—I'd live in that new place!

THE KITCHEN (pp. 66-67)

Conversation 1: *What's next?*

A: Your kitchen is so different from mine, Maria!
B: Well, there are some things that are the same.
A: Yes, we both have a refrigerator, a stove, and a sink. But you have a microwave. . . and a dishwasher.
B: I know. I love modern conveniences. I just bought an electric rice cooker!
A: Where will you put it? You don't have much counter space.
B: I'll find the space. I make rice every day.
A: You're a good cook, Maria. I remember that wonderful vegetarian dinner you cooked for me.
B: Well, you make a great sandwich!
A: That's about all I can make in my tiny kitchen. I eat out a lot. Hey, do you want to grab a bite to eat now?

Conversation 2: *What happened?*

A: What's your favorite room in your house, Erin?
B: Definitely the kitchen.
A: Really? Why?
B: When I was a child, the kitchen was the center of my family's life.
A: I remember that my mother was always busy in the kitchen.
B: Mine, too. And we all did our homework at the kitchen table.
A: So did we. It was great to be near the snacks!
B: My mother always kept an eye on us so we wouldn't fool around!

THE DINING ROOM (pp. 68-69)

Conversation 1: *What happened?*

A: Do you have a dining room in your house?
B: Are you kidding? I have a small apartment!
A: I meant, did you have a dining room when you were a child?
B: No, we didn't. Did you?
A: Yes. We ate dinner there every night.
B: What was it like?
A: It was pretty formal. It had a glass table and eight chairs. My mom taught us how to set the table. First, we always put a white tablecloth on the table. Then we put the plates, silverware, glasses, and napkins on the table.
B: Sounds pretty formal. We ate in the kitchen at a large, round table.
A: I bet you had more fun!

Conversation 2: *What's the process?*

A: Do you want to do the Group Role Play together?
B: Sure. Let's get three more. Carlos, do you want to be in our group?
C: Sure. How about Ted and Chet?
D: Sure.
E: All right.
A: OK, which scene should we choose?
C: Let's do the teenager one.
A, B, D, E: Sure. That's fine. Let's get started. What do we do first?
B: Well, what should the names be? How about Al? Jennifer?
C: Tiffany? Chuck?
D: And Pete? That's five.
E: OK. Now how do they feel? That's a weird question. What does it mean?
B: I think that means do they feel hungry or tired or happy or sad.
A: Right! Let's decide what they are going to say. . .

THE LIVING ROOM (pp. 70-71)

Conversation 1: *What's the process?*

Teacher: Time for the Class Game: "What do you do in the living room?" Write what you do on a piece of paper.
A: Let me see. What do I do? Hmm. . .
B: Oh, I know. . .
Teacher: OK everyone. Fold your papers. Now come up together. Make a pile of papers. Who wants to be first?
C: I do.
Teacher: OK, Jason. Pick one. Do a pantomime. Ask the class, "What am I doing?"
C: OK. What am I doing?
A: Listening to a CD.
C: Nope.
D: I know. He's studying and watching TV at the same time!
C: You guessed it! Your turn!

Conversation 2: *What's the process?*

A: Do we all have our ads from furniture stores for the Community Activity?
Students: Yes. I have mine! Yep.
A: Let's make a list of things for a living room. We'll start with a couch, OK?
B: And, of course, a stereo with a CD player!
C: Let's include a CD collection, too!
D: How about a TV? I know—an entertainment center! That includes the TV, VCR, and stereo.
E: How about two comfortable armchairs and a coffee table, too?

C: Let's add a nice rug and drapes.
B: Don't forget the lamps. And pictures for the walls!
A: We'd better stop here. Let's try to add up the bill. This is a pretty fancy living room!

THE BEDROOM (pp. 72-73)

Conversation 1: *What's the process?*

A: What was your childhood bedroom like?
B: Well, it wasn't very big. I shared it with my sister.
A: How many windows did it have?
B: It had one window. We had pink curtains on the window.
A: What furniture was in the room?
B: Let's see. We had our own beds, and each bed had a night stand. We each had our own desk, but we shared a dresser.
A: Was there a closet?
B: The closet! We had everything in that closet: games, dolls, toys, clothes, shoes. We also kept our secret letters and diaries there! And we never cleaned it! It was a mess!

Conversation 2: *What's happening?*

A: How many bedrooms are in your house?
B: We have three bedrooms: one for my parents, one for my two brothers, and one for me.
A: Tell me about your room.
B: It's a pretty big room. There's a blue bedspread on the bed and curtains to match.
A: Do you spend a lot of time in your room?
B: Oh, yes. I have a stereo and a TV. There's a carpet on the floor. It's very cozy.
A: You're lucky to have your own room. I share my bedroom with my younger sister. We have a telephone in our room, and we're always fighting over it.
B: Well, you're lucky to have a sister to fight with!

THE BATHROOM (p. 74)

Conversation: *What's happening?*

A: In the morning, the bathroom is the busiest room in our house!
B: That's because we're all rushing to get out in the morning. One bathroom is not enough!
C: OK, I've showered. I'll take my electric razor into the bedroom to shave. Next.
A: My turn!
D: No, mine!
B: Jenni, let your brother go first. He's faster! Take your toothbrush and toothpaste into the kitchen.
D: OK. I'm in a rush today. Just hurry up, Kevin!
A: I'll try, but I have to take a shower and wash my hair.
E: I have to use the toilet! I have to use the toilet!
B: I'll go last. I'm not working today. I'm going to take a nice bubble bath when you all leave!

AT HOME (p. 75)

Conversation: *What's the process?*

A: Time for a Group Survey, guys. Is everyone ready?
B: Let's try to get this one done. We never finish.
C: Is it OK if I ask the questions?
A, B, D: Sure. Fine. Let's get going.
C: How often do you eat lunch at home?
D: I never eat lunch at home.
B: I eat lunch at home every day. I live near the school.
A: Sometimes I eat at home, but sometimes I eat at school. I eat out a lot, too. I love sandwiches for lunch. That reminds me, I'm hungry.
C: Peter, you can eat later. We have to finish this survey!
Teacher: Time's up! Let's start to report back.

NEIGHBORS (pp. 76-77)

Conversation 1: *What's the process?*

A: Let's try this Partner Interview, Rex. I'll fill in your name and you fill in mine.
B: OK, Emi. You start asking the questions.
A: How many neighbors do you know?
B: I don't know any of my neighbors. They're very unfriendly. One has a big, ugly dog. I'm afraid of the dog and I'm afraid of the neighbor.
A: That's a shame. Is the dog on a leash?
B: No, it's not. That's why I'm afraid. I always think it'll bite me.
A: You know, my uncle lives near you—and he has a big German Shepherd named Killer.
B: Oh, no! That's the dog! That's my neighbor!

Conversation 2: *What's next?*

A: Are you still having problems with your next-door neighbors?
B: Yes, I'm afraid so. I just found out yesterday that their son, John, borrowed my son's bicycle without telling him.
A: That's terrible.
B: And now, Marge, John's mother, is gossiping to the other neighbors about us. She said that they lent my husband their snow shovel last winter, and he never returned it.
A: You're kidding. You always lend things to them!
B: I know. We always help them. I even baby-sat for John when he was a little baby.
A: I think you were too friendly to them—that's the problem.
B: I just know that I don't want to fight with them, but I have to do something about this problem!

PROBLEMS AT HOME (pp. 78-79)

Conversation 1: *What's happening?*

A: Mommy, Mommy! Come quick!
B: Just a minute, Stacy.
A: Mommy! The toilet is overflowing!
B: Oh, my goodness! The bathroom is flooded! Where's the plunger?
A: Mommy—here it is, behind the toilet!
B: Stacy, what did you put in the toilet?
A: Nothing, Mommy.
B: Nothing? What's this rubber ducky here? What a day!

Conversation 2: *What's next?*

A: I did my best with these pests. I don't know why you have so many cockroaches!
B: And the mice! This new apartment is a disaster.
A: Well, I sprayed a pesticide around the sink and under the counter. I think that's where the cockroaches are coming from.
B: What should I do about the mice?
A: Don't leave any food around. Try to keep all your food in plastice containers.
B: I know. The mice ate through a box of cereal.
A: And never leave dishes in the sink with food.
B: Yes, I found that out, too. The cockroaches just love my dirty dishes!

UNIT 6: SHOPPING

GOING SHOPPING (pp. 82-83)

Conversation 1: *What's your opinion?*

A: I love shopping at the mall! It's indoors, so it's always nice weather—cool in summer and warm in winter.
B: Exactly. Like today. It's raining out, but we don't need an umbrella!
A: There are so many shops here—and they all have great buys!
B: It's true. The best stores in town are here—Patterson's Department Store, The Jeans Outlet, that new CD store. . .
A: Yes, and the Bookmark. That bookstore is my favorite place in the mall!
B: My favorite is Munchie's Pet Shop. I always stop there.
A: Really? There's Munchie's now. Do you want to go in?
B: Sure. Oh, look at that cute little white doggie in the window! Isn't she adorable!
Little dog: Yap! Yap!

Conversation 2: *What's happening?*

A: Listen up, kids. You have one hour to shop. We'll meet back here at the mall coffee shop for lunch. One hour! Clear?
B, C: Yeah, yeah. Sure, Mom, one hour.
B: Let's check out the music store; OK, Mike?
C: Sure. Oh, wait a minute—nice weight set. I want that! I'm going to start lifting weights.
B: Yeah? You want to be a body builder, huh?
C: Right. . . Hey, take a look at those speakers! I bet they sound great. Man, they've got everything at that electronics store!
B: Come on, Mike. The music store, remember? I want to see if Loud Metal's new CD is out yet.
C: In a minute, in a minute. . . I really need a new pair of basketball shoes. Let's go back to the sporting goods store.
B: Mike! Let's go!
C: OK, OK. . .

SPORTING GOODS STORE (pp. 84-85)

Conversation 1: *What's next?*

A: May I help you, ma'am?
B: I hope so. My husband watches too much TV—he's a real couch potato. I think he needs a sport. What can I buy him?
A: Well, what sports does he like?
B: All sports. Every weekend he watches sports on TV all day—basketball, football, baseball, hockey, golf. Even soccer and bowling—he watches everything!
A: Hmm. . . Maybe he'd like golf. This nice set of clubs is on sale now. It's a very good price.
B: Oh, my! That's a good price? It's so expensive!
A: In that case, how about this nice starter set? It's not very expensive, and it has all the basic clubs.
B: Oh, that's a good idea! If he likes the set and enjoys playing, he can buy more clubs!

Conversation 2: *What's happening?*

A: You play baseball, don't you, George?
B: Yes, I do. I play every chance I get.
A: Where do you buy your baseball equipment?
B: There's a good sporting goods store downtown, Mickey's Sports. It has all kinds of athletic equipment. And it has pretty good prices, too.
A: Sounds good. My daughter wants to play baseball on a neighborhood team. What will she need?
B: Does she have a glove?
A: No, she's just beginning. She's only seven. She has a baseball cap, but that's all.
B: Well, she'll need a good glove. And maybe a bat and ball. She'll get the uniform with the team. I guess that's about it.
A: You've been a big help. Thanks, George!

TOY STORE (pp. 86-87)

Conversation 1: *What's your opinion?*

A: May I help you, sir?
B: Yes, thanks. My nephew is two years old today. I need to buy something for him.
A: What kinds of toys does he like?
B: I don't know. What do two-year-olds usually like?
A: How about a stuffed animal? We have some really cute ones here—the penguin? that big snake? a teddy bear, maybe?
B: Mmm. . . maybe. This tricycle is nice.
A: Yes, it is.
B: Do you think he might be too young for it? Oh, look at that little boy playing with the truck!
A: He looks about two years old.
B: Yeah, that's a great truck! My nephew will love it! I'll take it!

Conversation 2: *What's next?*

A: OK, kids, I want you to stay right with me! Susie? Where's Susie? Robert, where's your sister?
B: I don't know, Mommy.
A: She was right here a minute ago!
B: There she is, Mommy. She's in the toy store. See? She's playing with that paint set.
A: Oh, my goodness! Playing with a paint set! Hurry up, Robert—stay right with me! I don't want to lose you, too.
B: Oh, now she's pulling the dolls off the shelf! Is Susie a bad girl, Mommy? (*Bump!*)
C: Oh!
A: Oh, I'm sorry, Miss. Are you OK? My three-year-old ran away, and she's in the store here. . .
B: Mommy! Susie's climbed up, and she's playing with the computer! Uh-oh!
A: Oh, no!

SHOE STORE (pp. 88-89)

Conversation 1: *What's your opinion?*

A: Do you have a favorite pair of shoes, Tony?
B: I sure do, May. My old moccasins. They're so comfortable. I wear them all the time at home.
C: I have a pair of shoes like that—my old, suede loafers. I bought them a long time ago, and they fit perfectly. I love them.
D: I'm wearing my favorite shoes today—see?
A, B, C: Wow! Pretty nice! Fancy boots! They're beautiful!
D: They're real Western boots—handmade. I got them in Texas.
A: You all are lucky. I don't have any favorite shoes.
C: You don't?! Why not, May?
A: My shoes never fit right. My feet are wide, and the shoes are always too narrow. As a matter of fact, my feet hurt right now!

Conversation 2: *What's the process?*

A: Let's see, Find Someone Who. . . Brenda, do you have more than ten pairs of shoes?
B: I don't think so, Hiro. How about you?
A: No way! I don't think anybody does. It's a dumb question.
C: What do you mean, "a dumb question"? What's wrong with having more than ten pairs of shoes?
A: More than ten pairs? That's silly! Nobody needs that many shoes!
C: It doesn't seem silly to me.

B: How many pairs of shoes do you have, Molly?
C: Oh, I don't know. . . a few. . .
B: More than ten?
C: I'm not exactly sure how many. Let's see. I have a pair of walking shoes, and running shoes, and loafers, and then shoes for work—gray ones, and blue ones, and, of course, high heels—a black pair, and tan ones, and red ones, and white ones, and some flats, and my sandals, and do boots count? I have black boots, and red boots, and rubber boots. . .

MEN'S CLOTHING STORE (p. 90)

Conversation: *What's the process?*

A: I'm glad you're my partner for this interview, Frank. I don't know anything about shopping for men's clothing.
B: Well, to be honest, Lena, I don't know much about it, either.
A: You don't?! Why not?
B: My wife always buys my clothes for me.
A: Really? What about before you got married?
B: My mother shopped for me. I'm colorblind, so I don't see the colors right. If I buy my clothes, nothing looks good.
A: That's interesting, Frank. But, how can we answer these questions?
B: Why not just write our real answers? I don't think there are any "wrong" answers to these questions, Lena.

WOMEN'S CLOTHING STORE (p. 91)

Conversation: *What's happening?*

A: What's the matter, Jan? You look worried.
B: Oh, I don't know what to do. The party's tomorrow night, and I don't have anything to wear.
A: Why don't you try The Clothes Corner? It's a little dress shop at the shopping mall.
B: I don't think I know it.
A: You don't? Really? Oh, it has everything! Casual wear, sports clothes, bathing suits, hats—and wonderful party dresses!
B: Sounds like the store I need.
A: It's a wonderful store, Jan! Tell you what—let's go to the mall this afternoon. We'll check out The Clothes Corner.
B: And if I don't find anything there, we can look around. There are so many women's clothing stores at the mall.
A: Sure. Don't worry, you'll find something.

GRAMMAR FOR CONVERSATION

UNIT 1

VERB *TO BE*

Question

| Where | am / are / is / is / are / are / are | I / you / he / she / we / you / they | from? |

Affirmative

| You're / I'm / He's / She's / You're / We're / They're | from Africa. |

Negative

| You're not / I'm not / He's not / She's not / You're not / We're not / They're not | from Asia. |

PRESENT TENSE: REGULAR VERBS

Question

| Where | do / do / does / does / do / do / do | I / you / he / she / we / you / they | live? |

Affirmative

| You / I / He / She / You / We / They | live / live / lives / lives / live / live / live | in San José. |

Negative

| You / I / He / She / You / We / They | don't / don't / doesn't / doesn't / don't / don't / don't | live | there. |

PRESENT TENSE & SHORT ANSWERS

Question

| Do / Do / Does / Does / Do / Do / Do | I / you / he / she / we / you / they | have | a pet? |

Affirmative

| Yes, | you / I / he / she / you / we / they | do. / do. / does. / does. / do. / do. / do. |

Negative

| No, | you / I / he / she / you / we / they | don't. / don't. / doesn't. / doesn't. / don't. / don't. / don't. |

IMPERATIVES
Affirmative–Negative

| Look! | Don't look. |
| Guess! | Don't guess. |

Affirmative–Negative

| Tell. | Don't tell. |
| Write. | Don't write. |

DEMONSTRATIVE PRONOUNS: THIS/THAT/THESE/THOSE

This	is my photo.
That	is your photo.
These	are my sisters.
Those	are your parents.

THERE IS/THERE ARE

| There is | one teacher. |
| There are | twenty students. |

INTERROGATIVES
Question

What	is your name?
Who	is he?
Where	do you live?
How many	students are there?

Answer

My name is Sue.
He's my brother.
I live in Arizona.
There are 15 students.

PRESENT CONTINUOUS TENSE
Question

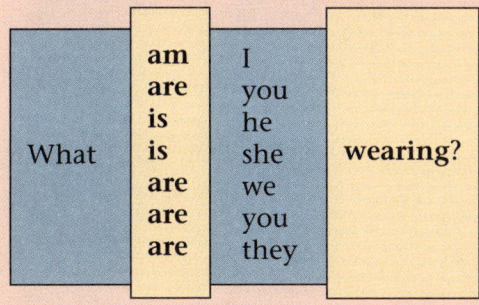

Affirmative

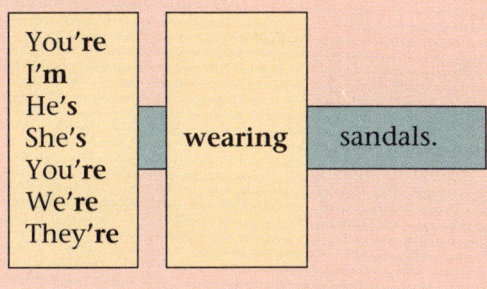

Negative

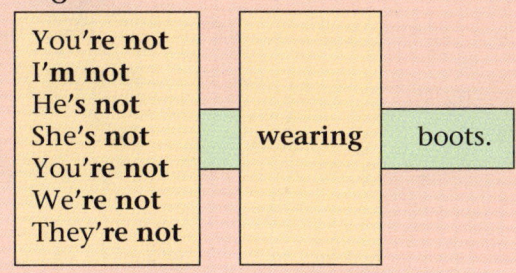

107

POSSESSIVES

Possessive Adjective

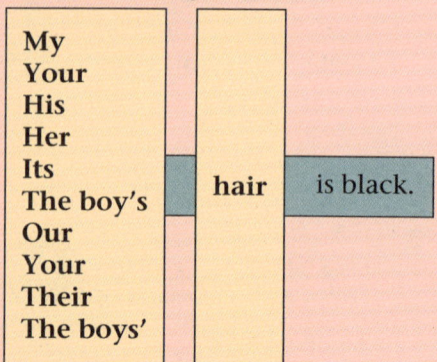

Possessive Pronoun

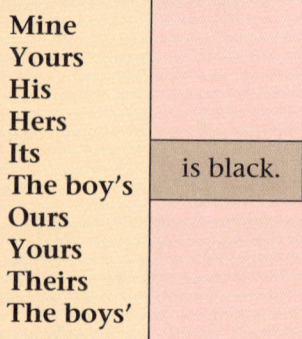

IRREGULAR NOUNS

Singular	Plural
1 child	2 children
1 man	2 men
1 woman	2 women
1 wife	2 wives

UNIT 2

ADJECTIVES

He's hungry. / thirsty. / sick. / happy. / tired.

He's a hungry / thirsty / sick / happy / tired man.

ADVERBS & OTHER EXPRESSIONS OF FREQUENCY

When do you go to class?
When does she study?
How does he work?
How does he eat?
How does she read?

I go / She studies / He works / He eats / She reads — early. / late. / hard. / slowly. / fast.

How are you?
What time do you get up?
How often do you watch TV?
What about Sally?
How about this?

I always / usually / never get up early.

I get up early every day. / every morning. / sometimes.

PHRASAL VERBS

Oh, hi! **Come in.**
I **get up** early.
I **get out of** bed right away.
I **get dressed** quickly.
He **gets ready** for work fast.
I **go to** bed late.
She **looks like** her sister.

They **punch in** at work.
They **punch out** after work.
Please, **sit down.**
Sit up, please.
Don't **stand up.**
He **wakes up** late.

DO/MAKE

do the dishes   make the bed
do the laundry   make coffee
do the shopping   make dinner
do homework   make friends
do housework   make my day

PREPOSITIONS

The students are **in** the classroom.
The clock is **on** the wall.
He's coming **into** the room.
Their feet are **under** the table.
She eats dinner **at** home.
She goes **to** school.
He gets **out of** bed.
He leaves **for** work.

SET PHRASES

Hey!
Oh, my!
You, too?

UNIT 3

PAST TENSE: *TO BE*

Question

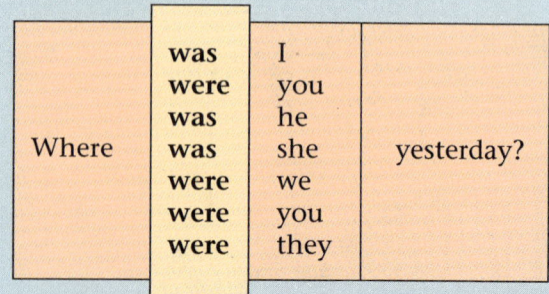

Affirmative

You	were	
I	was	
He	was	at home.
She	was	
You	were	
We	were	
They	were	

Negative

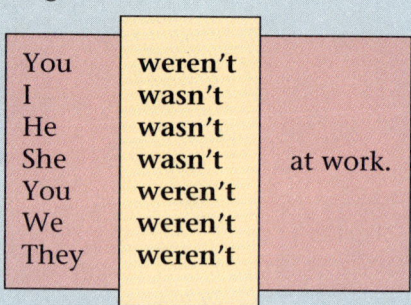

PAST TENSE: REGULAR VERBS

Question

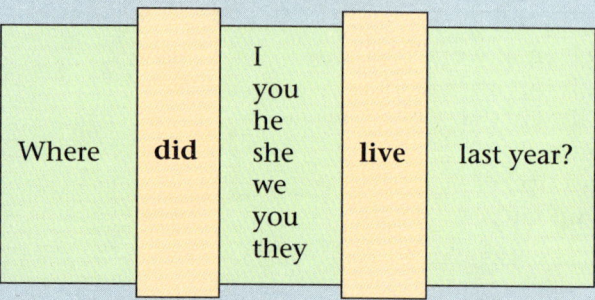

Affirmative

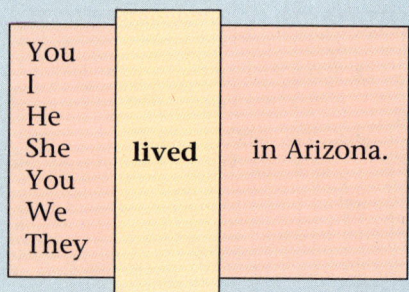

Negative

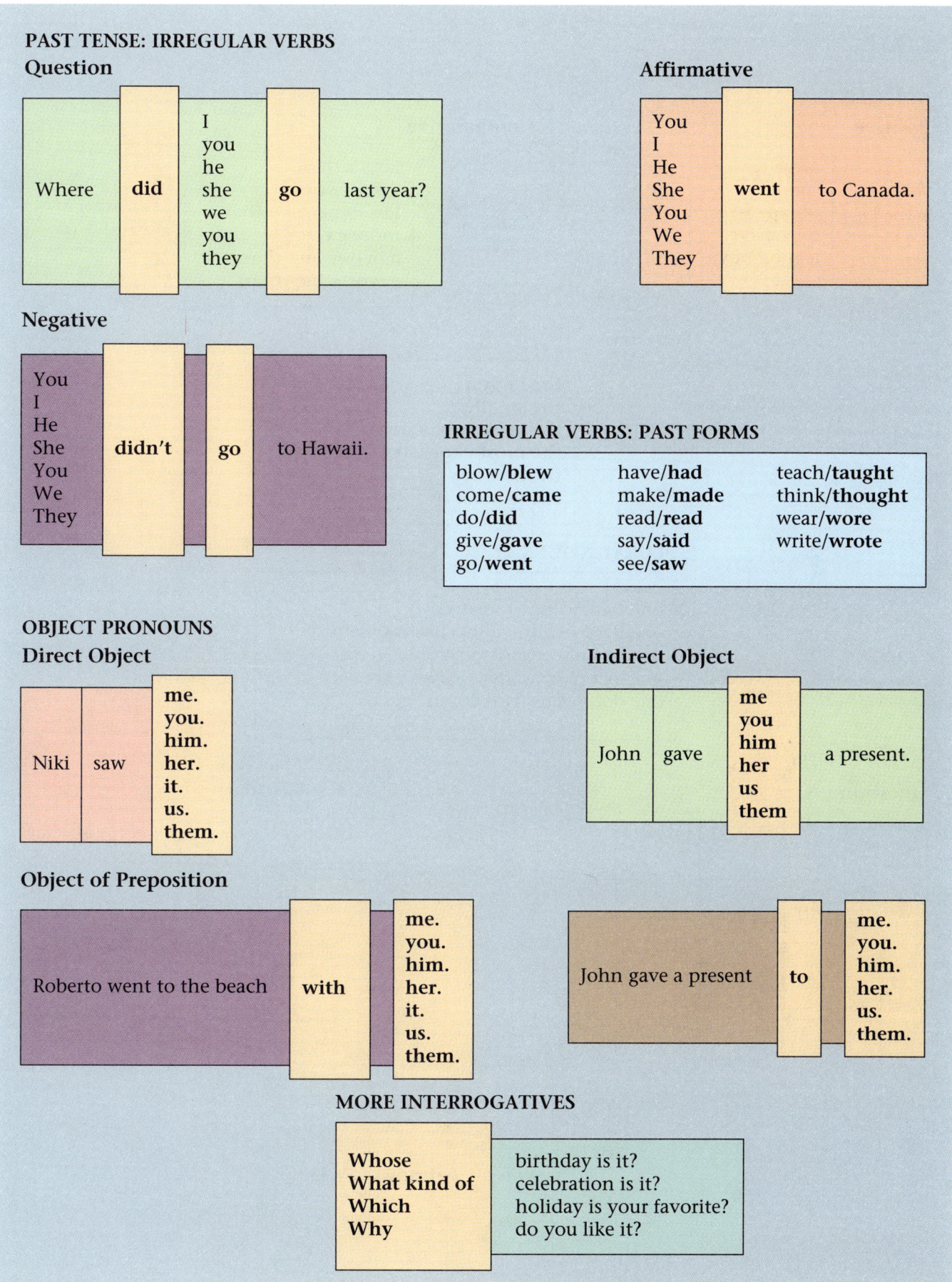

UNIT 4

ADJECTIVES

Positive

The jar is | large. / small. / inexpensive. / expensive. / a good buy.

Comparative

This jar is | larger than / smaller than / less expensive than / more expensive than / a better buy than / a worse buy than | the other one.

Superlative

This jar is | the largest / the smallest / the least inexpensive / the most expensive / the best buy / the worst buy | of all.

PLURAL NOUNS

one tomato/two tomatoes
one head of lettuce/two heads of lettuce
one box of cereal/two boxes of cereal
one loaf of bread/two loaves of bread
one dozen eggs/two dozen eggs

FUTURE: WILL

Question

What | will | I / you / he / she / we / you / they | bring?

Affirmative

You'll / I'll / He'll / She'll / You'll / We'll / They'll | bring | a fork.

Negative

You / I / He / She / You / We / They | won't | bring | a knife.

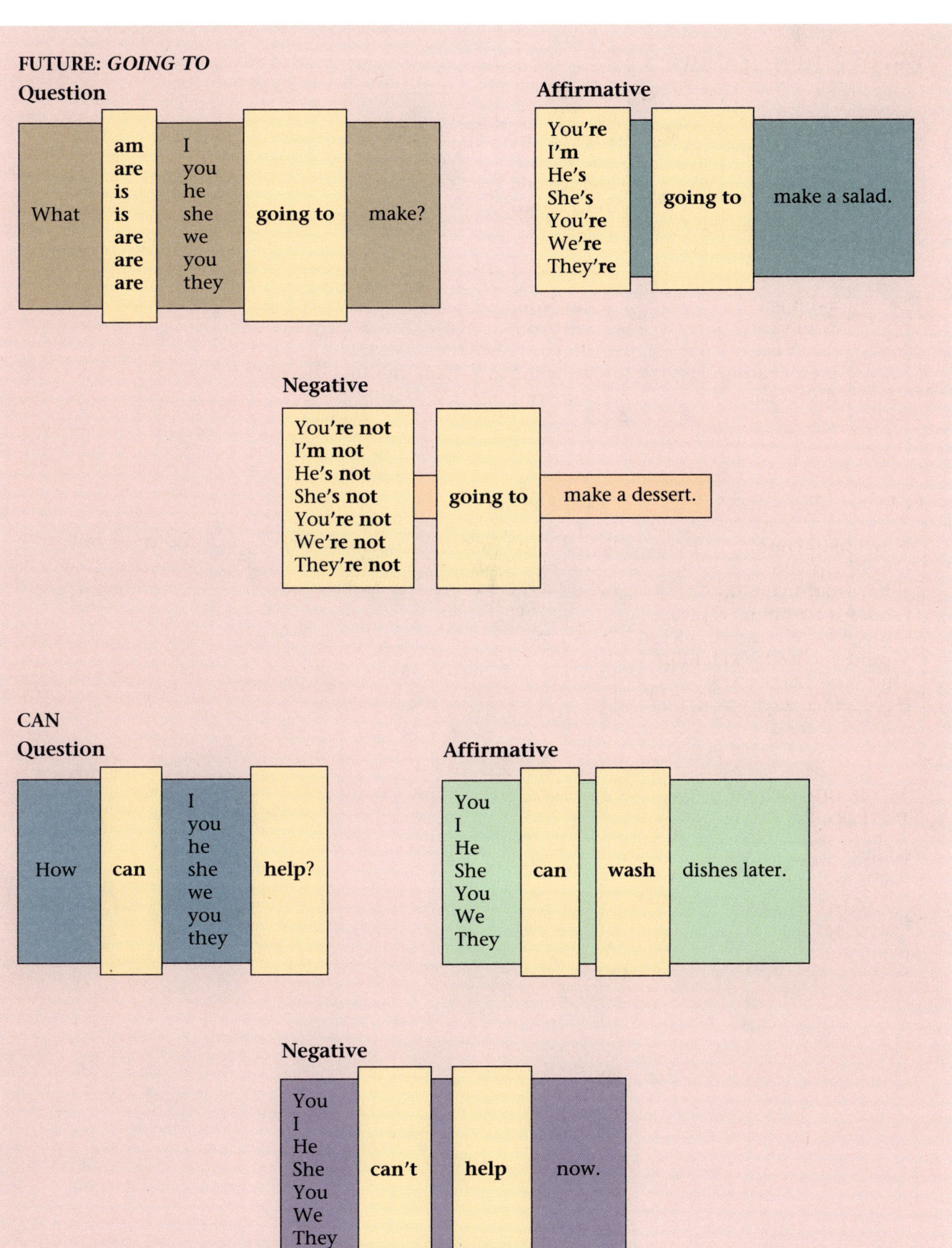

TAG QUESTIONS & ANSWERS

You | can eat / will eat / eat / are eating / ate | lunch, | can't you? / won't you? / don't you? / aren't you? / didn't you? | Yes, I can. / Yes, I will. / Yes, I do. / Yes, I am. / Yes, I did.

You | can't eat / won't eat / don't eat / aren't eating / didn't eat | lunch, | can you? / will you? / do you? / are you? / did you? | No, I can't. / No, I won't. / No, I don't. / No, I'm not. / No, I didn't.

POLITE EXPRESSIONS

May I help you?
Can I help you?
What would you like?
I'd like a hamburger, please.
Could I have mustard, please.
Would you prefer ketchup?
That'll be $2.00.
Have a nice day!   You, too!

SET PHRASES

By the way. . .   Lucky you!   Wish me luck!
Here it is!   That's too bad!   You bet.
I can't wait!   What a surprise!   You name it!
Let see. . .

MORE IRREGULAR VERBS: PAST FORMS

bring/**brought**
buy/**bought**
eat/**ate**
lose/**lost**
put/**put**

UNIT 5

PRESENT PERFECT TENSE: REGULAR VERBS

Question

| How long | have / have / has / has / have / have / have | I / you / he / she / we / you / they | lived | there? |

Affirmative

| You've / I've / He's / She's / You've / We've / They've | lived | there since June. |

Negative

| You / I / He / She / You / We / They | haven't / haven't / hasn't / hasn't / haven't / haven't / haven't | lived | there very long. |

FOR/SINCE

| I've lived in Seoul | for | a little while. / two years. / a long time. |

| I've lived in Seoul | since | last November. / 1985. / I was four years old. |

SHOULD

Question

| What | should | I / you / he / she / we / you / they | do? |

Affirmative

| You / I / He / She / You / We / They | should | turn off | the water. |

Negative

| You / I / He / She / You / We / They | shouldn't | do | that! |

SET PHRASES

Are you kidding?	Let me see...	What a day!
at all	Now, what?	Wow!
I guess so.	Oh, my goodness!	You guessed it!
I'm afraid so.	So did we.	

PHRASAL VERBS & IDIOMS

eat out	grab a bite to eat
fill in	keep an eye on
fool around	

UNIT 6

PRESENT PERFECT TENSE: IRREGULAR VERBS

Question

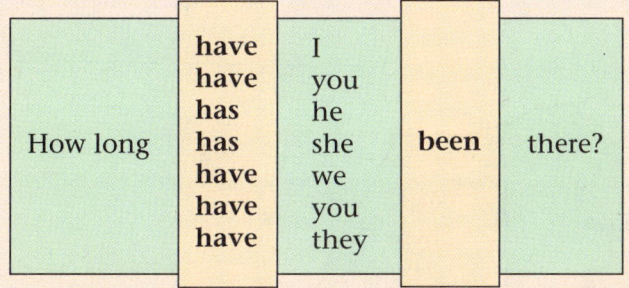

How long | have/have/has/has/have/have/have | I/you/he/she/we/you/they | been | there?

Affirmative

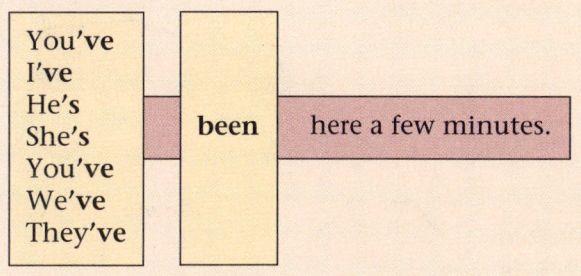

You've/I've/He's/She's/You've/We've/They've | been | here a few minutes.

Negative

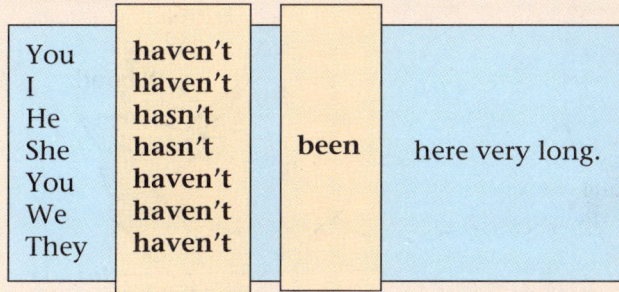

You/I/He/She/You/We/They | haven't/haven't/hasn't/hasn't/haven't/haven't/haven't | been | here very long.

IRREGULAR VERB FORMS

Simple	Past	Past Participle
be	was/were	been
bring	brought	brought
buy	bought	bought
cost	cost	cost
go	went	gone
have	had	had
make	made	made
pay	paid	paid
spend	spent	spent
take	took	taken
wear	wore	worn

SET PHRASES

Check out. . .   I sure do.   That's about it.
Clear?   Let's go!   That's right.
Come on.   Like today.   To be honest. . .
Don't worry.   Listen up.   Uh-oh!
Exactly.   Oh, no!   Wait a minute.
I bet. . .   Really?   What's the matter?
I hope so.   Right!   Why not?
I'll take it!   Take a look. . .
I'm sorry.   Tell you what. . .

MAY

Question

May I help you?
May I ask a question?
Where will you go shopping?
What will you buy?

Answer

Yes, thanks. I'd like to try on some shoes.
Yes, of course. What is it?
Well, I **may** go to the mall, but maybe not.
I'm not sure. I **may** not buy anything.

AFRICA

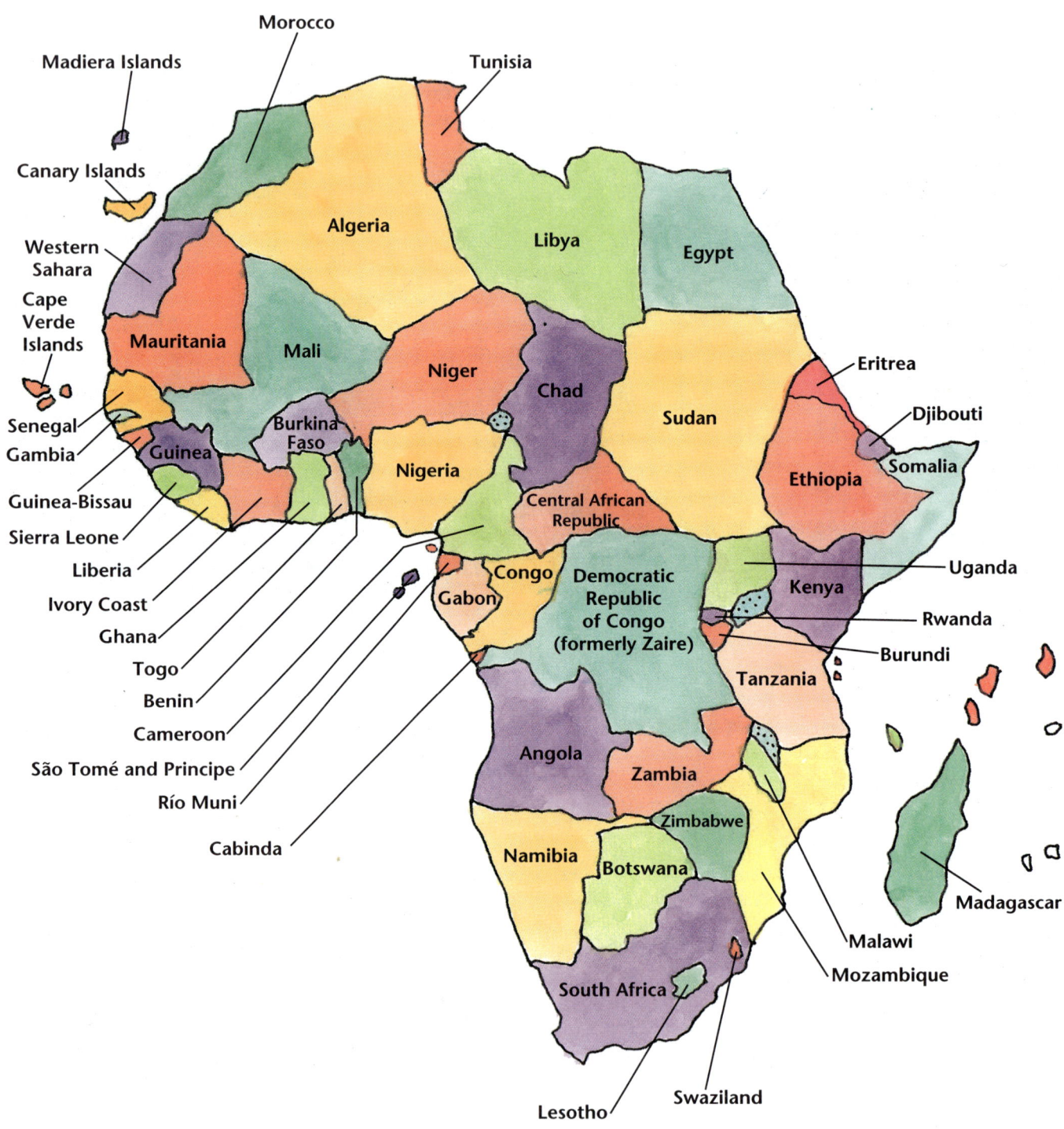

ASIA AND AUSTRALIA

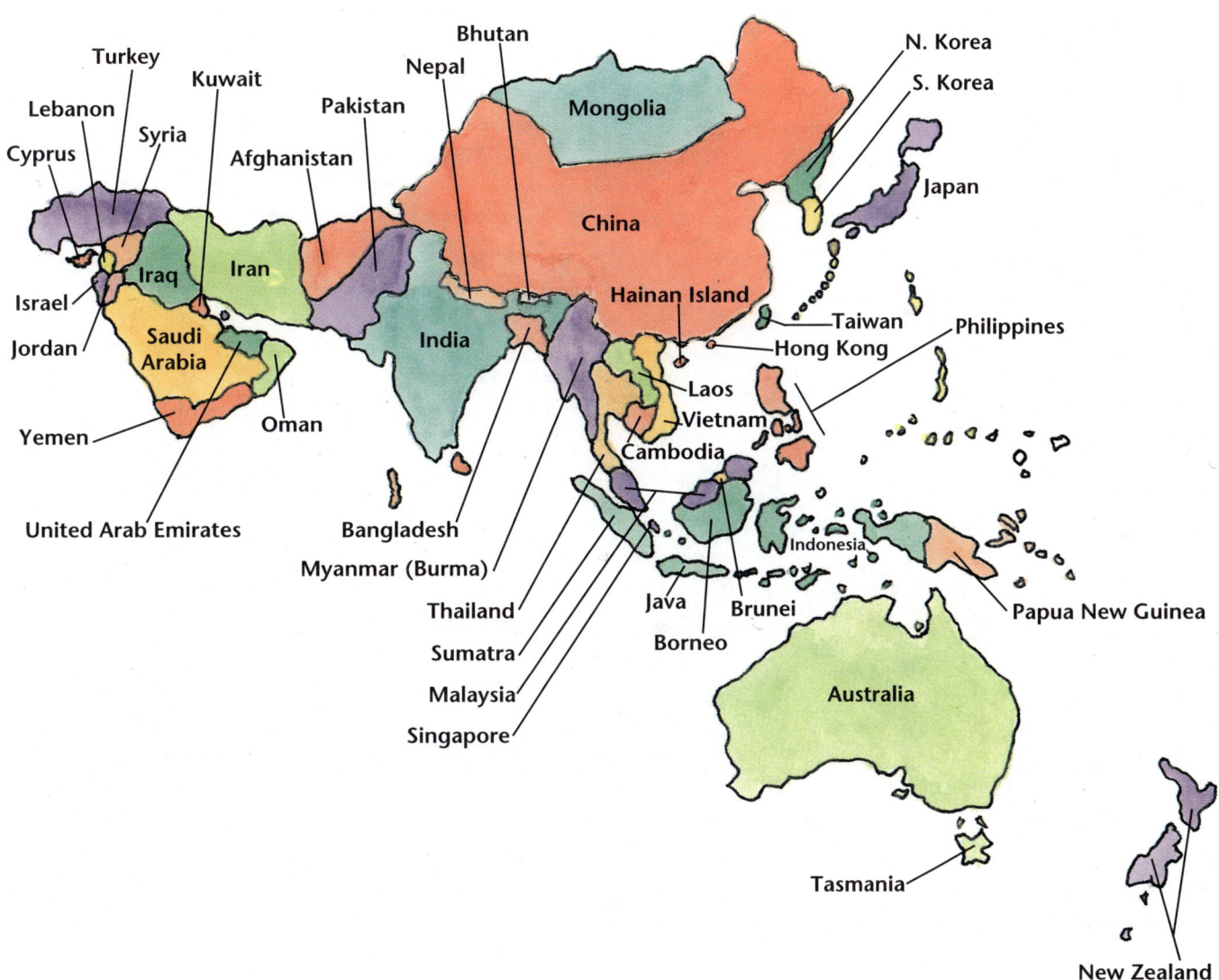

119

EUROPE

NORTH AMERICA, CENTRAL AMERICA, AND SOUTH AMERICA

121

UNITED STATES OF AMERICA (U.S.A.) AND CANADA

NATIONS/NATIONALITIES

Notice that many nationalities end in *-ese, -ian, -ish, -an*, or *-i*.

NATION	NATIONALITY	NATION	NATIONALITY
	(-ese)		(-an)
China	Chinese	Chile	Chilean
Japan	Japanese	Costa Rica	Costa Rican
Lebanon	Lebanese	Cuba	Cuban
Portugal	Portuguese	The Dominican Republic	Dominican
Senegal	Senegalese		
Sudan	Sudanese	Kenya	Kenyan
Taiwan	Taiwanese	Korea	Korean
Vietnam	Vietnamese	Mexico	Mexican
		Puerto Rico	Puerto Rican
	(-ian)	South Africa	South African
Argentina	Argentinian	Uganda	Ugandan
Australia	Australian	United States of America	American
Brazil	Brazilian		
Canada	Canadian	Venezuela	Venezuelan
Egypt	Egyptian		
Ethiopia	Ethiopian		(-i)
Haiti	Haitian	Israel	Israeli
Hungary	Hungarian	Kuwait	Kuwaiti
India	Indian	Pakistan	Pakistani
Indonesia	Indonesian	Saudi Arabia	Saudi
Iran	Iranian	Somalia	Somali
Italy	Italian		
Lithuania	Lithuanian		(irregular)
Nigeria	Nigerian	France	French
Panama	Panamanian	Germany	German
Peru	Peruvian	Greece	Greek
Romania	Romanian	Netherlands	Dutch
Russia	Russian	Switzerland	Swiss
		Thailand	Thai
	(-ish)		
Denmark	Danish		
England	English		
Ireland	Irish		
Poland	Polish		
Spain	Spanish		
Sweden	Swedish		
Turkey	Turkish		

NAMES/NICKNAMES

Notice that some men's and women's nicknames are the same or have the same pronunciation. Many nicknames for children end in -y. Some names do not have nicknames. Add more names to the list.

MEN

GIVEN NAME	NICKNAMES
Albert	Al, Bert
Alexander	Alex, Al
Alfred	Al, Fred
Andrew	Andy, Drew
Anthony	Tony
Arnold	Arnie
Brian	_____
Christopher	Chris
Daniel	Dan, Danny
David	Dave, Davey
Edward	Ed, Eddie, Ted, Teddy
Eugene	Gene
Francis	Frank, Frankie
Gerald	Gerry, Jerry
James	Jim, Jimmy
Jason	Jay
Jeffrey	Jeff
John	Jack, Johnny
Joseph	Joe, Joey
Joshua	Josh
Justin	_____
Lawrence	Larry
Lee	_____
Louis	Lou, Louie
Mark	_____
Martin	Marty
Matthew	Matt, Matty
Melvin	Mel
Michael	Mike, Mikey
Nathaniel	Nat
Nicholas	Nick, Nicky
Patrick	Pat
Paul	_____
Peter	Pete, Petey
Richard	Dick, Rich, Rick, Ricky
Robert	Bob, Bobby, Rob, Robbie
Scott	Scotty
Sean, Shawn	_____
Stephen, Steven	Steve, Stevie
Terence	Terry
Theodore	Ted, Teddy
Thomas	Tom, Tommy
William	Bill, Will, Billy, Willy

WOMEN

GIVEN NAME	NICKNAMES
Abigail	Abby
Alison, Allison	_____
Andrea	Andy, Andi
Ann, Anne	Annie
Ashley	_____
Barbara	Barb, Barbie
Carol, Carole	_____
Carolyn	_____
Catherine	Cathy
Christine	Christie, Tina, Chrissy, Chris
Cynthia	Cindy
Dorothy	Dot, Dottie
Elaine	_____
Elizabeth	Beth, Betsy, Betty, Liz
Emily	Em, Emmy
Faith	_____
Fay, Faye	_____
Frances	Fran
Gail	_____
Gloria	_____
Heather	_____
Helen	_____
Hope	_____
Jacqueline	Jackie
Jane	_____
Janet	Jan
Janice	_____
Jean, Jeanne	Jeannie
Jeanette	_____
Jessica	Jess, Jessie
Joan	Joannie
Joanne	Jo
Judith	Judy
Kathleen	Kathy
Laura	_____
Laurie	_____
Linda	_____
Lisa	_____
Margaret	Peggy, Peg, Maggie
Martha	Marty
Mary	_____
Maryanne	_____
Nicole	Niki
Patricia	Pat, Patty, Patsy
Rebecca	Becky
Roberta	Bobbie
Rose	Rosie
Sally	Sal
Sandra	Sandy
Sharon	Sherry
Stephanie	Steph
Susan	Sue, Susie
Teresa, Theresa	Terry, Terri

GOSSIP SECRETS

UNIT 5, PAGE 63: *City or Country*

I was born and grew up on a farm in the country. It was very peaceful and beautiful. Then I went to the city with my husband. I did not like the city. It was too noisy and crowded. Now my family and I live in a town in the mountains. We are happy there.

UNIT 5, PAGE 71: *Living Room*

I love my living room. I stay in the living room all day. Sometimes I lie on the sofa and watch TV. Sometimes I listen to music and sleep in the armchair. Sometimes I walk on the coffee table and eat the plant there. I like to play with the pillow on the sofa and the lampshade on the lamp. I am a beautiful yellow cat.

SPEECH EVALUATION FORM

Speaker's Name: _____
Date: _____
Speech Topic: _____

	Needs Work	Satisfactory
Organization	_____	_____
Pronunciation	_____	_____
Vocabulary	_____	_____
Eye Contact	_____	_____
Visual Aids	_____	_____

Best Part of Speech: _____
Recommendations: _____

Evaluator's Name: _____

AUDIENCE EVALUATION FORM

Speaker's Name: _____
Date: _____
Speech Topic: _____

	Needs Work	Satisfactory
Attentiveness	_____	_____
Quietness	_____	_____
Eye Contact	_____	_____
Appropriateness of Questions	_____	_____
Form of Questions	_____	_____
Number of Questions	_____	_____
Responsiveness	_____	_____

Recommendations: _____
_____

Evaluator's Name: _____

NOTE: Make as many copies of these forms as you need.

ALPHABETICAL WORD LIST TO PICTURE DICTIONARY

A

activity, 33
adult, 10
Africa, 4
afternoon, 18
ago, 26
aisle (supermarket), 58
a la mode, 48
alarm clock, 18
always, 51
a.m., 18
angry, 17
apartment (flat), 64
apple, 42
apple pie, 33
appliances (small), 66
apricot, 42
April, 28
argue, 16
armchair, 70
artichoke, 44
ash tray, 57
Asia, 4
aspirin, 74
athletic (equipment), 84
Atlantic Ocean, 4
attic, 64
August, 28
aunt, 10
autumn (fall), 34
awning, 64

B

baby, 20
baby shoes, 88
baby-sit, 76
bacon, 50
bag (golf), 84
    (shopping), 91
bagel, 50
baggie (plastic), 52
bake, 47
balcony, 64
bald, 2
ball (bowling), 84
    (golf), 84
    (soccer), 84
balloon(s), 30
banana, 42
band, 32
bandaid(s), 74
bar (candy), 56
    (chocolate), 56
    (salad), 54
barbecue, 47
barrette, 8
baseball, 84
    (bat), 84
    (cap), 84
    (glove), 84
basement, 64
basil, 47
basketball, 84
bat, 84
bathing suit, 39
bathrobe, 90

bathroom, 74
bath towel(s), 74
bath toy(s), 74
bathtub, 74
beach, 34
beach towel, 34
bean, 44
beard, 2
beautiful, 62
bed, 18
bedroom, 72
bedspread, 72
beef (ground), 46
    (roast), 46
    (stew), 46
beer, 57
beet, 44
belt, 8
bench, 36
beverage, 48
bicycle, 86
bikini, 39
bill (amount), 71
bird, 34
birthday(s), 30
birthday cake, 30
black, 2
blackberry, 42
blanket, 72
blond, 2
blouse, 8
blow out (the candles), 30
blue, 2
blueberry, 42
board (chalkboard), 14
board game(s), 86
boil, 47
boiled ham, 52
bologna, 52
book, 14
    (read), 70
bookcase, 70
boots, 9
    (Western), 88
    (winter), 88
    (work), 88
borrow, 76
bother, 76
bottle, 58
bottle return, 58
bowl (cereal), 50
    (salad), 68
    (soup), 68
    (sugar), 66
bowling ball, 84
box, 42
    (lunch), 52
boxer shorts, 9
box spring, 72
boy, 2
bra (brassiere), 91
brand (name), 59
bread, 52
break (time out), 16
breakfast, 18
brick, 64
broccoli, 44
broil, 47

brother, 10
brother-in-law, 10
brown, 2
brownie(s), 48
brown paper bag (sack), 52
brush, 72
brush (his teeth), 22
bubble bath, 74
bubble gum, 56
bun, 54
bunch (of grapes), 42
burner, 66
busboy, 57
busy, 62
butter, 50
button, 8
buy, 42

C

cabbage, 44
cabinet (kitchen), 66
    (medicine), 74
cactus, 36
cactus garden, 64
cafe (coffee shop), 82
cafeteria, 52
cake, 30
calendar, 26
calm, 62
can, 46
candle(s), 30
candlestick(s), 68
candy, 48
candy bar, 56
can opener, 66
can return, 58
cantaloupe, 42
canvas, 88
cap, 90
    (baseball), 84
    (stocking), 39
cappuccino, 48
car (toy), 86
carpet, 72
carrot, 44
carton, 58
cashier, 54
cash register, 54
casserole, 47
casual wear, 90
cat, 10
CD player, 70
ceiling, 14
celebrate, 30
celery, 44
cement, 64
Central America, 4
century, 28
cereal, 50
cereal bowl, 50
chair, 14
chalk, 14
champagne, 32
change (money), 54
chat, 76
cheap, 88
check, 57

checkout counter, 58
cheese, 52
    (cream), 50
    (grated), 58
cheesecake, 48
cheese snack(s), 56
cherry, 42
chess set, 86
chest of drawers, 72
chicken, 46
chicken nuggets, 54
children (child), 10
chili, 47
chimney, 64
chocolate bar, 56
chocolates, 32
chops, 46
    (lamb), 46
    (pork), 46
Christmas, 33
Christmas lights, 33
cider, 34
city, 4
class, 2
classroom, 14
clear, 36
cleats, 84
clock(s), 14
    (alarm), 18
    (digital), 18
clock radio, 18
closet, 72
clothing, 8
clothing rack, 91
cloud(s), 36
cloudy, 38
club (golf), 84
coast, 62
coat, 8
cockroach(es), 78
cocoa, 50
coconut, 42
coffee, 22
    (iced), 48
coffee cake, 48
coffee maker, 66
coffee mug, 52
coffee shop (cafe), 82
coffee table, 70
cold, 17
cold cut(s), 52
collar, 8
color(s), 8
comb (his hair), 22
come in, 16
computer (games), 86
conditioner (hair), 74
condominium, 64
cone, 48
continent, 4
cook(ed) (vegetables), 45
cookies, 48
cool, 38
cooler, 34
corn, 44
corn chip(s), 56
costume (Halloween), 32
couch (sofa), 70

126

third (3rd), 28
thirsty, 17
thirteen, 6
thirteenth (13th), 28
thirtieth (30th), 28
thirty, 6
thirty-first, 28
this week, 26
three, 6
throw pillow, 70
thunder, 36
thunderstorm, 36
Thursday, 26
tie, 8
tights, 91
tile(s), 74
time, 18
tip, 57
tired, 17
toast (French), 50
toaster, 66
today, 26
toilet, 74
    (stopped up), 78
toilet paper, 74
toilet seat, 74
tomato, 44
tomato paste, 58
tomato sauce, 58
tomorrow, 26
toothbrush, 74
toothpaste, 74
tortilla chips, 56
towel (bath), 74
    (beach), 34
    (hand), 74
toy(s) (bath), 74
toy kitchen, 86
toy store, 82
tree, 33
Trick or Treat!, 32
tricycle, 86
truck (toy), 86
try on, 91

T-shirt/tee shirt, 8
Tuesday, 26
tulip, 34
tuna, 46
tuna fish, 46
turkey, 33
turtleneck, 90
twelfth (12th), 28
twelve, 6
twentieth (20th), 28
twenty, 6
twenty-eight, 6
twenty-eighth (28th), 28
twenty-fifth (25th), 28
twenty-first (21st), 28
twenty-five, 6
twenty-four, 6
twenty-fourth (24th), 28
twenty-nine, 6
twenty-ninth (29th), 28
twenty-one, 6
twenty-second (22nd), 28
twenty-seven, 6
twenty-seventh (27th), 28
twenty-six, 6
twenty-sixth (26th), 28
twenty-third (23rd), 28
twenty-three, 6
twenty-two, 6
two, 6

U

umbrella, 36
uncle, 10
undershirt, 90
underwear, 39
unfriendly, 76

V

Valentine's Day, 32
vanity, 72
vase, 68

VCR
    (videocassette recorder), 70
vegetable(s), 44
vending machine, 56
vest, 39
volleyball, 34

W

waiter, 57
waitress, 57
wake up, 18
walk, 16
walking shoes, 88
wall, 14
wallet, 90
warm, 36
wash(es) (the dishes), 20
washing machine, 66
wastebasket, 14
watch (jewelry), 18
watch (the news), 22
    (TV), 70
water, 34
    (glass), 57
watermelon, 42
wave, 16
wavy, 2
weather, 36
weather map, 38
weather report, 38
Wednesday, 26
week (last), 26
    (next), 26
    (this), 26
weekday, 26
weekend, 26
welcome, 2
west, 38
Western boots, 88
wet, 36
whipped cream, 58
whisper, 76
white, 8

wide (W), 88
widowed, 2
width, 88
wife, 10
wind, 36
window, 14
windy, 38
wine, 57
winter, 34
winter boots, 88
wise, 11
wish, 30
witch, 32
wok, 66
woman, 2
women, 6
women's clothing, 82
women's clothing store, 82
wood, 64
work(s), 20
work boots, 88
worker, 20
world, 4
worry, 16
write, 5

X

Y

yard, 64
yawn, 16
year, 28
yellow, 8
yes, 19
yesterday, 26
yogurt, 52
    (frozen), 48
young, 11

Z

zero, 6
zipper, 8

puck (hockey), 84
puddle, 36
pumpkin, 32
punch, 30
punch(es) in, 20
purple, 8

Q

R

rack (clothing), 91
    (hat), 91
radiator (heat), 78
radio, 70
    (clock), 18
rain, 36
raincoat, 8
rainy, 38
raise (your hand), 14
rake, 34
ranch, 62
raspberry, 42
raw, 45
razor (electric), 74
read, 16
reads (a book), 70
    (the newspaper), 22
    (to the children), 20
recipe, 53
red, 8
reel (fishing), 84
refrigerator, 66
register (cash), 54
relax, 70
report (weather), 38
restaurant, 57
restroom, 57
return (can), 58
    (bottle), 58
rice, 58
roast, 47
roast beef (sandwich), 46
robe, 91
rod (fishing), 84
roll, 52
roof, 64
    (leaking), 78
room (dining), 68
    (living), 70
routine (morning), 22
rubber(s,)39
rubber ball, 86
rubber boot(s), 88
rug, 70
rural, 62

S

sack/brown paper bag, 52
saddle, 36
sage, 47
salad, 52
salad bar, 54
salad bowl, 68
salad dressing, 54
salami, 52
salsa (hot sauce), 54
salt, 47
salt shaker, 68
same, 21
sandals, 9
sandwich, 52
Santa Claus, 33
Saturday, 26
sauce (spaghetti), 52

saucer, 68
sausage(s), 46
say (goodbye), 22
scarf, 8
school, 20
seafood, 46
season(s), 34
seasonal clothing, 39
seasoning, 47
second (2nd), 28
    (part of minute), 18
secret, 76
section, 58
    (nonsmoking), 57
    (smoking), 57
seeds, 42
September, 28
serving spoon, 68
set (the table), 68
settlers, 33
seven, 6
seventeen, 6
seventeenth (17th), 28
seventh (7th), 28
seventy, 6
shade, 72
shake, 54
shaker, 68
    (pepper), 68
    (salt), 68
shake hands, 16
shampoo, 74
shave, 22
shaving cream, 74
sheet(s), 72
shelf, 58
sherbet, 48
shirt, 8
shiver, 78
shoe(s), 9
shoe box, 88
shoe horn, 88
shoe polish, 88
shoe size, 88
shoe store, 82
shoe tree(s), 88
shop, 82
shopping, 20
shopping bag, 91
shopping cart, 58
shopping center, 82
short (hair), 2
    (person), 11
shorts (boxer), 9
    (jockey), 9
short sleeves, 90
shoulder pads, 84
shower (bathe), 22
shower (rain), 38
shower curtain, 74
shred(ded), 45
shrimp, 46
siblings, 10
sick, 17
silver, 8
silverware, 68
simmer, 47
single, 2
single parent, 10
sink, 66
sister, 10
sister-in-law, 10
sit, 16
six, 6
sixteen, 6
sixteenth (16th), 28

sixth (6th), 28
sixty, 6
size(s), 88
skate(s) (ice), 34
ski(s), 84
ski boots, 84
ski jacket, 39
skin (fruit), 42
ski pants, 39
ski poles, 84
skirt, 8
slacks (pants), 91
sled, 34
sleep, 16
sleeve(s), 90
slice(d), 45
slice of bread, 52
slicker, 39
slip, 91
slippers, 9
small appliance, 66
small (S) (size), 90
smile, 16
smoking section, 57
snack(s), 56
snack machine, 56
snake (toy), 86
sneakers (tennis shoes), 9
snow, 34
snowball, 34
snowflake(s), 38
snowman, 34
snowstorm, 36
soap, 74
soap dish, 74
soccer, 84
    (ball), 84
    (shoes), 84
socks, 9
soda, 56
    (ice cream), 48
sofa (couch), 70
soft drink, 54
sole (shoe), 88
sometimes, 26
son, 10
soup, 52
soup bowl(s), 68
south, 38
South America, 4
southeast, 38
southwest, 38
spaghetti, 52
spaghetti sauce, 52
speak, 16
speaker(s) (electronic), 70
splash, 36
spoon(s), 30
sporting goods, 82
sporting goods store, 82
sports coat, 8
spring, 34
stand, 16
stationery, 82
stationery store, 82
steak, 46
steam, 47
steps (home), 64
stereo, 70
stew beef, 46
stick (hockey), 84
stir fry, 47
stocking(s), 9
stocking cap, 39
stopped up (plugged up), 78
store, 82

    (department), 82
    (electronics), 82
    (hardware), 82
    (jewelry), 82
    (men's clothing), 82
    (music), 82
    (shoe), 82
    (sporting goods), 82
    (stationery), 82
    (women's clothing), 82
storm (dust), 36
story, 30
stove, 66
straight (hair), 2
straw(s), 54
strawberry, 42
streamers, 32
stucco, 64
student, 14
study, 18
stuffed animal(s), 86
submarine (hero/grinder), 52
suburban, 62
suede, 88
sugar, 50
sugar bowl, 66
suit, 8
suit (bathing), 39
summer, 34
sun, 36
sundae, 48
Sunday, 26
sunglasses, 9
sunny, 38
sunshine, 36
supermarket, 58
surprise, 30
sweater, 8
sweat pants, 90
sweatshirt, 8
sweatsuit, 84
sweep(s) (the floor), 20
swim trunks, 39
swordfish, 46
sympathetic, 11
syrup, 50

T

table, 14
    (coffee), 70
tablecloth, 68
tablespoon, 68
tag (price), 91
take(s) (a break), 16
    (a shower), 22
talk, 16
tall, 11
tank top, 39
tea, 48
teacher, 14
tea kettle, 66
teaspoon, 68
teddy bear, 86
tee (golf), 84
teeth, 22
telephone, 72
television/TV, 70
temperature, 38
ten, 6
tenth (10th), 28
terrace, 64
Thanksgiving, 33
thermos, 52
thin, 11
think, 5

I love you, 32
Independence Day, 32
in-laws, 10
international, 49
island, 4
item, 59

J

jacket, 8
jack-o'-lantern, 32
jam, 50
January, 28
jar, 58
jeans, 9
jelly, 50
jewelry, 82
jewelry store, 82
jockey shorts, 9
journal, 7
juice (drink)(s), 56
    (orange), 50
July, 28
June, 28
jungle, 62
junk food, 56

K

ketchup, 52
kitchen, 66
    (toy), 86
kiwi, 42
knife, 30

L

lamb chops, 46
lamb roast, 46
lamp, 70
lampshade, 70
language, 4
large (L) (size), 90
laser disk player, 70
last (week), 26
late, 18
laugh, 16
laundry, 20
leaf (leaves), 34
leak, 78
leaking roof, 78
leap year, 28
leather, 88
leave (for work), 22
leftovers, 52
leg of lamb, 46
lemon, 42
lemonade, 48
lend, 76
length, 88
lettuce, 44
life, 13
lightning, 36
lights (Christmas), 33
lime, 42
line, 54
linoleum, 66
listen, 16
    (to music), 70
live, 62
liver (meat), 46
living room, 70
loaf, 58
loafer(s), 88
lobster, 46
long, 2
long sleeves, 90

long underwear, 39
look, 16
lunch, 18
lunchbox, 52
lunchroom, 52

M

machine, (washing), 66
magazine, 70
maitre d', 57
make(s) (a pile), 5
    (a wish), 30
    (dinner), 20
    (the bed), 22
mall, 82
man, 2
mango, 42
man made materials, 88
map, 4
    (weather), 38
March, 28
margarine, 50
married, 2
mat, 74
material(s), 88
mattress, 72
May, 28
mayonnaise, 52
meat (crab), 46
meatballs, 46
medicine cabinet, 74
medium, (M) (size), 90
men, 6
men's clothing, 82
men's clothing store, 82
menu, 49
Merry Christmas!, 33
meteorologist, 38
microwave oven, 52
midnight, 18
midwest, 38
mild, 38
milk, 50
milkshake, 48
mint, 47
minute (part of hour), 18
mirror, 72
mittens, 9
mobile, 86
mobile home, 64
mocassin(s), 88
model airplane(s), 86
Monday, 26
month(s), 28
morning, 18
motel, 65
mother, 10
mother-in-law, 10
mountain(s), 62
mouse, 78
moustache, 2
muffin, 50
mug, 52
mushroom, 44
music, 82
music store, 82
mustard, 52

N

name, 2
nap, 36
napkin(s), 68
    (paper), 30
narrow (N), 88

Native Americans, 33
neighbor(s), 76
nephew, 10
nervous, 17
nest, 34
never, 51
new, 9
news, 22
newspaper, 22
New Year's Eve, 32
next, 26
next door, 76
next week, 26
nice, 11
niece, 10
night, 18
nightgown, 91
night stand, 72
nine, 6
nineteen, 6
nineteenth (19th), 28
ninety, 6
ninth (9th), 28
no, 19
noisy, 62
nonsmoking section, 57
noon, 18
north, 38
North America, 4
northeast, 38
northwest, 38
no smoking, 57
notebook, 14
November, 28
nuggets (chicken), 54
number, 6

O

oatmeal, 50
October, 28
octopus, 46
off, 78
old (person), 11
old (thing), 9
on, 78
one, 6
one hundred, 6
onion, 44
on time, 18
open, 5
orange, 42
orange juice, 50
order, 54
oven, 66
    (microwave), 52
overflow, 78
oz. (ounce), 58

P

Pacific Ocean, 4
package, 46
pad(s) (shoulder), 84
paint, 86
paint set, 86
pair(s), 9
pajamas, 9
pan (frying), 66
pancakes, 50
panties, 9
pants (slacks), 9
pantyhose, 9
papaya, 42
paper, 14
    (napkin)(s), 30
    (toilet), 74

paper bag, 52
paper plate(s), 30
parade, 32
parent(s), 10
party, 30
party hat, 30
paste (tomato), 58
pastry, 48
pay, 54
paycheck, 20
peaceful, 62
peach, 42
peanut(s), 56
peanut butter, 52
pear, 42
peas, 44
peel(ed), 45
pen, 14
pencil, 14
penguin (toy), 86
pepper, 44
pepper shaker, 68
pest(s), 78
pesticide, 78
pet(s), 10
pharmacy, 82
photo, 11
photograph, 70
pickle, 54
picnic, 36
picture, 2
pie, 48
    (apple), 33
pie a la mode, 48
pie server, 68
pig's feet, 46
pile, 5
Pilgrims, 33
pillow, 72
    (throw), 70
pillowcase, 72
pineapple, 42
pink, 8
pit, 42
pitcher, 68
place, 4
plant (green), 70
plastic, 88
plastic baggie, 52
plate(s), 68
    (paper), 30
plow, 34
plugged up (stopped up), 78
plum, 42
plunger, 78
p.m., 18
pocket, 8
point, 14
poncho, 39
popcorn, 56
porch, 64
pork chops, 46
portrait, 11
pot (cooking), 66
potato, 44
potato chips, 52
poultry, 46
pound, 42
present(s), 30
pretzel(s), 56
price, 59
price tag, 91
prison, 64
private home, 64
problem(s), 76
produce, 44

counter, 54
    (checkout), 58
countries (nations), 4
country (rural), 62
courtesy desk, 58
cousin, 10
cowboy, 36
crab meat, 46
cracker(s), 56
cream, 50
    (shaving), 74
    (whipped), 58
cream cheese, 50
creamer, 66
crowded, 62
cry, 16
cucumber, 44
cup(s), 30
cupboard, 66
curly, 2
curtains, 72
    (shower), 74
customer, 54
cutoffs, 39

D

Danish, 50
darts, 86
date(s), 28
daughter, 10
day, 20
day after tomorrow, 26
day before yesterday, 26
December, 28
Declaration of Independence, 32
decorations, 32
deodorant, 74
department, 82
department store, 82
desert, 62
desk, 14
    (courtesy), 58
dessert(s), 48
different, 21
digital clock, 18
dill, 47
dining room, 68
dinner, 18
dish(es), 20
    (soap), 74
dishpan, 66
dishwasher, 66
divorced, 2
do(es) (homework), 20
    (laundry), 20
dog, 10
doll, 86
door, 14
doorknob, 14
dormitory, 64
doughnut, 48
dozen, 58
drain, 74
drapes, 70
draw, 16
drawer, 72
dress, 8
dressed, 22
dresser, 72
dress shirt, 90
drink(s) (beverage)(s), 56
    (coffee), 22
    (soft), 54
drip, 78

drive-in/drive thru window, 54
dry, 38
dryer, 66
duck (toy), 86
dust storm, 36

E

ear (of corn), 44
early, 18
earmuffs, 39
earrings, 2
east, 38
eat (breakfast), 18
    (dinner), 18
    (lunch), 18
egg, 34
    (fried), 50
eight, 6
eighteen, 6
eighteenth (18th), 28
eighth (8th), 28
eighty, 6
electric mixer, 66
electric razor, 74
electric train(s), 86
electronics, 82
electronics store, 82
eleven, 6
eleventh (11th), 28
engine (fire), 86
entree, 52
equipment, 84
erase, 16
eraser, 14
espresso, 48
Europe, 4
evening, 18
every day, 26
everyday, 13
exciting, 62
expensive, 88
exterminator, 78
extra large (XL) (size), 90
eye(s), 2

F

fall (autumn), 34
family, 10
farm, 62
farm market, 44
farm stand, 34
fast food, 54
father, 10
father-in-law, 10
faucet, 66
favorite, 11
February, 28
feed(s) (the baby), 20
fence, 64
fifteen, 6
fifteenth (15th), 28
fifth (5th), 28
fifty, 6
fight, 76
fire engine, 86
fireplace, 70
fireworks, 32
first (1st), 28
fish, 46
fishing, 84
fishing reel, 84
fishing rod, 84
fit (clothing), 88

five, 6
flag, 32
flat (apartment), 64
flat(s) (shoes), 88
flooded, 78
floor, 14
flower(s), 32
flower stand, 82
fly (flies), 84
    (fishing), 84
fold, 5
food, 33
football, 84
fork(s), 30
forty, 6
four, 6
fourteen, 6
fourteenth (14th), 28
fourth (4th), 28
freezer, 66
freezing, 78
French toast, 50
fresh, 44
Friday, 26
fried egg, 50
friendly, 76
frown, 16
frozen, 59
    (entree), 52
frozen yogurt, 48
fruit, 42
fry, 47
frying pan, 66
funny, 11
furniture, 70

G

garage, 64
garden, 34
    (cactus), 64
get(s) (a paycheck), 20
get dressed, 22
get out of bed, 22
get up, 18
ghost, 32
gift(s), 30
girl, 2
glass, 68
glass (of water), 57
glasses (eye), 2
globe, 14
glove(s), 9
    (baseball), 84
go(es) out, 16
    (shopping), 20
    (to bed), 18
    (to class), 18
    (to school), 20
    (to work), 20
gold, 8
golf, 84
golf (bag), 84
    (ball), 84
    (club(s), 84
    (tee(s), 84
goodbye, 22
gossip, 76
grandfather, 10
grandmother, 10
grandparents, 10
grape, 42
grapefruit, 42
grass, 36
grated cheese, 58
gray, 2

green, 2
grinder (hero/submarine), 52
grits, 50
ground beef, 46
grow (up), 62
guess, 5
gum (bubble), 56

H

hail, 36
hailstorm, 36
hair, 2
Halloween, 32
halter, 39
ham, 46
    (boiled), 52
    (sandwich), 52
hamburger, 54
hand (shake), 16
handkerchief, 8
hand towel, 74
happy, 17
Happy Birthday!, 31
Happy Halloween!, 32
Happy New Year!, 32
Happy Valentine's Day!, 32
hardware, 82
hardware store, 82
harvest, 34
hat rack, 91
have (a party), 76
head (of lettuce), 44
headband, 91
heat, 78
heavy, 11
heel (shoe), 88
helmet, 84
help, 76
helpful, 11
hero (submarine/grinder), 52
hide, 30
high heels, 88
hill, 36
hockey, 84
    (puck), 84
    (skates), 84
    (stick), 84
holiday(s), 32
holiday activity, 33
holiday food, 33
home(s), 61
    (mobile), 64
    (private), 64
home fries, 50
homework, 20
horn(s), 30
horse, 36
hosiery, 91
hostess, 57
hot, 17
hot dogs, 46
hot sauce (salsa), 54
hour, 18
house, 64
hungry, 17
husband, 10

I

ice, 34
ice cream, 48
ice-cream soda, 48
iced coffee, 48
iced tea, 48
ice skates, 34